Inside The World's Top Institutional Investment Offices

Conversations With
80 Institutional Investors

A Trusted Insight Production

Written & Edited by
Ian Floyd, Sissi Cao

CONTENT

Part V: Selected Trusted Insight Exclusive Interviews:

Inside The World's Top Institutional Investment Offices

Conversations With
80 Institutional Investors

Foreword

It is 10 years since Cathleen Rittereiser and I embarked on our project to write a book on the investment approaches of 12 leading foundation and endowment investors. A lot has happened since we wrote our book. Global stock markets experienced a 50 percent drawdown during the 2008-2009 financial crisis, followed by the second longest bull market in the S&P 500 since WWII. Bond yields reached record lows. All institutional investors or asset owners experienced the pain of the downturn, followed by the long recovery in markets and asset prices.

There was a need for a new book, which looks at the current issues faced by the investment offices of endowments and foundations and extends this to a broader group of asset owners, including family offices, health systems, pensions and sovereign wealth funds. *Inside The World's Top Institutional Investment Offices* does a great job of detailing the investment processes and philosophies pursued by a range of asset owners. The authors estimate that 4,400 investment offices oversee over $40 trillion of aggregate asset value. The authors interviewed 80 investment office professionals, providing a window into the backgrounds of these investors, their investment processes, the management of their teams and portfolios, and the challenges they face in the current environment. This book is valuable for anyone trying to: seek a career at one of these investment offices, start an investment office, provide board oversight to an investment office or forge a relationship with one of these institutions. The book is also ideal for the classroom. For years, I have taught applied investment classes. This book will be perfect supplemental reading the next time I teach my class.

I have a number of observations and important takeaways from the book.

People

I am honored to be a colleague of the investors profiled in this book. They are serious investment professionals who are constantly accountable for their investment performance. Ana Marshall, CIO of the Hewlett Foundation, observes that you are only as good as your numbers. Investment officers must be able to answer the question, "Can you deliver?"

There was not a single "normal" career path followed by these 80 people, although many had economics and finance majors and earned CFA designations. Some had science and engineering backgrounds, including Sean Feng, who earned a Ph.D. in pharmacology and is a former biopharmaceutical researcher. Alan Chang, at Capricorn Investment Group, majored in electrical engineering, computer science and art history. He credits the science majors for logic and analytical rigor, but credits his art history background for helping him identify top-down trends. Many of the investment office professionals are former investment bankers, consultants, accountants and direct investors, but the group also includes a former lawyer, realtor and U.S. Naval officer.

Many interviewees stressed that investing is a people business, and that people grow and develop through apprenticeship. Many recommend being intellectually curious and a continuous learner. Yup Kim of the Alaska Permanent Fund advises to "be a voracious reader."

Team

The Investment Offices have a range of sizes and structures. At one end of the spectrum is Steve Edmundson, who is the one-person investment office for the Nevada Public Employees Retirement System. He emphasizes the benefit of discipline and patience. The authors explore alternative organizations between those that favor generalist, specialist or hybrid staffing models. Many stressed the importance of sharing ideas across the team and portfolio. Some noted that the boundaries between asset classes and strategies are weakening. I often find that some of the most interesting ideas are "tweeners", which don't fit neatly into a bucket. Elizabeth Hewitt, CIO of the Alfred P. Sloan Foundation, says, "I think that people who work across these areas have a great advantage in learning and becoming a well-rounded asset allocator and investor." Many stressed the value of building a team that has a diversity of backgrounds and views.

Portfolio and Current Opportunities

The authors start with the Investment Policy Statement, stating that this is the DNA of any investment organization. It sets the governance and decision-making process. It is helpful for achieving a long-term mindset, which will enable the institution to ride out short-term market volatility. The profiled institutions have a range of delegated decision-making frameworks. Many noted that there are a variety of different investment philosophies and approaches, but that it is important to maintain a consistency over time to avoid chasing the latest investment fads. Robert Maynard, the long-time and successful CIO at the Public Employee Retirement System of Idaho, says, "There are a thousand ways to invest … the key is to find the best way given the institution's history and traditions. I put a high premium on explainability."

The investment professionals often spoke of the need to be creative and independent thinkers. Stuart Mason, the successful CIO of the University of Minnesota, is a great example of being independent. They focus their entire effort on finding alpha or excess performance from private investments, preferring passive investments for their public portfolio. Stuart provides detail on how they select investment managers and where they are focusing their efforts in the today's environment. Many investors expressed the challenge of finding returns in such an environment given current valuations and the competition for investing capital with talented investment managers. Many investors are more interested in emerging markets because of better valuations and the better opportunity for alpha. Stuart Mason mentioned that over half of their fixed income is in "go-where-banks-don't-go" strategies. Investors are seeking niche strategies (e.g., water), credit investments (in particular lending strategies), considering direct or co-investing, and some are focused on cutting high fees for declining alpha. One investor noted, "There are too many hedge fund and private equity managers … and second tier managers will disappear." Another investor noted that "alpha is ephemeral." Those that continue to use active and alternative investment managers look for an investment edge as well as honesty and transparency. Colin Ambrose, CIO of the UJA Federation of New York, said he looks for "intelligence coupled with ethics."

Concluding Thought

A common description of the ideal investment manager is that of a long-term partner. The most consistent theme of the book is that investing is a people business. Long-term success is strongly influenced by the quality of the people within the investment office as well as the quality of the people at the investment firms with whom they partner.

Lawrence E. Kochard
May 30, 2017

Introduction

In September 2015, Trusted Insight embarked on the ambitious task of interviewing the world's top institutional investors. To date, we spoke to more than 150 chief investment officers, directors and investors of varying seniority from endowments, foundations, pension funds, family offices, sovereign wealth funds, hospital systems and corporations in the United States and across the globe.

While we humbly admit that we have much ground to cover, Trusted Insight has accumulated a mass of knowledge about this complex, often secretive and constantly evolving industry. The pages that follow are the culmination of 18 months of dialogue chronicling and dissecting the institutional investor psyche and the resulting decisions through which an investment office's strategy, process and identity are constructed.

Institutions diverge wildly in terms of size, structure, culture and capital needs, but all are bound by an inherent long-term perspective and a reliance on talented teams to execute their mission. To that end, Trusted Insight organized answers from 80 of the best interviews to chronicle the career paths, teams, investment strategies and the current trends driving an industry that controls more than $40 trillion.

This book is not intended to be an in-depth analysis of institutional investment. Instead, this is an oral history, a snapshot of an industry expanding and adapting amid market forces unlike any in our lifetimes. It is with great honor that we present *Inside The World's Top Institutional Investment Offices*.

Part I

CAREER PATH

Institutional investing is a challenging profession. The field is crowded by the brightest individuals with backgrounds spanning a spectrum of disciplines. Some are in it for the money, others wish to impact the world, but everyone has a common love for investing. As David Holmgren, the chief investment officer of Hartford Healthcare, said, "whether we're nice or not, we're all very competitive individuals, or we shouldn't be in the investment industry."

Bartley Parker, the managing director of real estate at Maine Public Employees Retirement System, said, "successful people in this business seek to find out why something is, not just what it is, and I've always enjoyed asking the question 'why?'"

To articulate such an explanation takes years of rigorous and continuous education through both formal channels and real-world experience investing through various market cycles and regulatory environments. Ultimately, investment is a people business. The fate of projects across the world -- research at top universities, pension checks for countless retirees, state-of-the-art equipment for hospital systems, charitable gifts toward addressing Earth's largest dangers and inequalities -- comes down to people and their ability to synthesize a lifetime of information and relationships into a coherent, stable and efficient portfolio.

In this opening chapter, we profile institutional investors not just as capital allocators, but as individuals with unique life stories. You will learn what attracted them to this profession, what they did to prepare for the career, how they entered the industry and all the obstacles and struggles one is bound to face along the way.

1. Becoming An Institutional Investor

Institutional investment offices around the world control an immense amount of capital, but the stewards of this money operate in a very small circle. Trusted Insight estimates that there are between 25,000 to 28,000 limited partners and approximately 80,000 asset managers worldwide.

From chief investment officers to portfolio managers, institutional investors come from diverse academic and professional backgrounds. Among the 80 investment professionals Trusted Insight interviewed for this book since September 2015, we have observed a few common characteristics: a majority have undergraduate degrees in science-related fields; many are former asset managers, investment bankers and accountants; there is a small group of investors who spent their early work years in non-finance fields, but later took a dramatic turn in career paths -- many of which have unorthodox, yet inspiring insights on how a non-finance background can actually help one become a savvy investor.

Preponderance Of Science Degrees

Education is the bedrock for any career. When we surveyed educational backgrounds of our interviewees, we found that a majority studied science or science-related subjects in college, such as math, biology and physics. Many noted the benefits of a science education in making investment decisions.

Sean Feng, an investment director at Kresge Foundation, a $3.6 billion private foundation based in Troy, Michigan, was a biopharmaceutical researcher for seven years before entering the investment world. Originally from China, Feng graduated from Nankai University, one of the most prestigious research universities in China, in the early 1990s with a bachelor's degree in biochemistry.

Like many top-tier science students of his generation, in 1996, he pursued higher education in the United States. Feng attended the University of Texas at

Austin to pursue a Ph.D. degree in pharmacology, but found himself drawn to economics and finance. "Once in the U.S., I soon began to be fascinated by the economy and the market, which were quite different from what I experienced in China. Wanting to understand them, I started listening to The Marketplace (NPR) and reading the Wall Street Journal and still wanted to learn more. In the end, I decided to change my career," Feng said.

Feng discontinued his doctoral study and left the University of Texas with a master's degree in pharmacology. He then worked for DuPont as a biotechnology researcher while self-teaching finance for five years. In 2003, he was admitted into the MBA program at the University of Chicago's Booth School of Business, majoring in analytic finance and entrepreneurship.

Upon graduation from business school, Feng went to work in fundamental stock research, first at Citigroup Smith Barney and later at NorthPointe Capital, an asset manager focused on U.S. small- and mid-cap stocks.

Feng's foundation in science played a critical role in guiding his investment thought process. "My background in science taught me to ask basic questions and to develop my own perspectives rather than blindly following others," he said. "There are a lot of similarities between fundamental scientific research and investing. Independent thinking is critical for both fields. In science, I read extensively, formed an independent hypothesis and then designed experiments to test my hypothesis. The same process can be applied to the investment world."

Feng joined Kresge Foundation in 2011 as an investment director. He works on a 14-person generalist team, which means each team member has responsibilities for managers in multiple asset classes and geographies. Developing an approach that would suit a broad range of investments is challenging, and that's where "asking basic questions" comes into play.

"I tried different investment approaches. Eager to find the approach that fits me, I read many books and forced myself to think deeply about my own investment philosophy. In the end, I found that long-term focused, fundamental-based value investing philosophy resonates best with me."

"When looking at different industry sectors, asset classes or different countries, I also try to focus on basic questions and to build my own frameworks to guide investment. For example, when evaluating technology investments, I will first step back and try to understand the fundamental nature of investing in technology companies: their business models and cyclicality, tried and tested best practices for investing in the technology sector. Breaking problems down to their first principles often leads to very different solutions," he said.

James Perry, former chief investment officer at Dallas Police & Fire Pension System, also attributed his investment philosophy to his earlier education in science. Perry graduated from the University of Houston with a degree in biochemistry and biophysics. "I think there's a huge value in taking a scientific approach when investing," he said. "I was taught and trained in the scientific method to build an understanding of how things work: you start out with a hypothesis, but continue to question, challenge and refine the idea. I think it's a good foundation for an investor. "

After College, Perry went on to pursue an MBA from the National University. He said that while one can learn a great deal about markets, the fundamental rules of investing and financial modeling from business school, having studied science teaches a higher of level thinking that forces you to "question what we think we know."

Perry described himself as a "dynamic investor," with the constantly fluctuating price of assets as the central factor driving his investment decisions. "I know there are a lot of folks who take a more static view on asset allocation. I would be considered more of a dynamic investor. I adhere to the premises that an investor should always ask if they are being compensated for the risk of any investment and that relative value considerations can improve asset allocation decisions," he said. He documented this philosophy in a 2012 academic paper "Dynamic Beta: Getting Paid to Manage Risks," which he co-authored with three peer investors. The paper received the Edward D. Baker III Journal Award from the Investment Management Consultants Association in April 2012.

In July 2016, Perry left Dallas Police & Fire Pension System to join Maples Fund Services, a global fund service provider, as head of institutional investor solutions.

Lorrie Tingle, chief investment officer at the Public Employees' Retirement System of Mississippi, said science degrees are common among institutional investors.

Tingle studied geology in college and worked as an exploration geologist for seven years before switching her career path to finance. She started at the retirement fund in 1991 as an investment analyst and worked her way to chief investment officer in 1996. "Many people I meet in this business have backgrounds in engineering, math and science. The analytical training you get in those fields of study is a perfect foundation for work in this business," she said.

Yet, Tingle emphasized the importance of preparation for a career in investments through continued higher education, such as MBA and CFA programs. "You've got to have the business fundamentals to understand what makes markets work and what makes companies successful or unsuccessful investments. I think an MBA is definitely beneficial. I'm also a big believer in the CFA program. It provides a strong foundation in investment theory and helps you master many of the concepts associated with finance and investment management," she said.

Ron Virtue, the director of investments at JM Family Enterprises, a Florida-based automotive company, said that the benefit of early scientific training is underappreciated by most people. Virtue graduated from the University of Michigan in 1995 with a bachelor's degree in actuarial mathematics and statistics. "I don't think a lot of people realize this, but higher math is really right-brain thinking. When you come up through the lower math, that's very left-brain thinking. But once you reach higher math you need to be able to combine those different parts of your mind," he said. "The thought process that I learned in the actuarial math program taught me how to solve problems and analyze."

Despite the preponderance of science degrees in institutional investing, there are a number of other areas of study that underlie successful investors. Alan Chang, a partner and managing director at Capricorn Investment Group, triple majored in electrical engineering, computer science and art history in college. He found that what he had learned in all these three areas -- art history in particular -- shaped his professional identity and investment philosophy. "Clearly, the study of the fifth-century Buddhist art probably doesn't fit in specifically. I think the benefit of a liberal arts education is that it teaches you how to learn," Chang said. "[Art history] lends that macro lens that allows me to look at trends. In very simple words, art history was about connecting the dots. It's using different works of art at different periods and finding the connection and reading the trends between them."

Using the fifth-century Buddhist art as an example, he said, "Buddhism was spread from India to China. Overall, the Buddhist statues were changing from a very Greco-Roman style to an Indian style and then to a much more Chinese style. It was about noticing how things change over time, mapping those and trying to find a connection and see a trend."

"Art history gives that top-down approach, while electrical engineering and computer science allow for the logical thinking. This allows for building systems and very technical due diligence. These skills are still being used today."

The similar influence of liberal arts is found by Anne-Marie Fink, chief investment officer of the Employee Retirement System of Rhode Island, who has a bachelor of arts in humanities from Yale University. "[A liberal arts degree] has been enormously helpful, mostly in the ability to synthesize," Fink said. "We would study different eras of history, mostly European history, and look at them through different prisms or disciplines -- through history, literature, philosophy and art. It required thinking about the common threads that you find across all of those different disciplines. That is similar to what you do in investing. You look at what's happening with rates, in equities, in macroeconomic indicators and try to pull together a cohesive view of the markets and where opportunities lie."

Diverse Investment Backgrounds

During our interviews, we found that most investors, regardless of academic backgrounds, went through formal finance education programs, such as CFA and MBA, and spent their first years working in various capacities before embarking on institutional investment. The most common areas of previous experience include investment banking, accounting, asset management and investment consulting.

Dean Duchak, a director of investments at Kaiser Family Foundation, a private foundation based in Menlo Park, California, was a trader at J.P. Morgan for two years before joining Kaiser in 2011. Duchak studied finance and accounting at Georgetown University. Upon graduation, he was admitted into a rotational development program at J.P. Morgan. "Leaving school and going to work for a big bank like J.P. Morgan on Wall Street feels like you get tossed into the deep end," he recalled of his first impression of the bank as a fresh college graduate. "It creates that exponential learning curve where you are getting up to speed as fast as possible. To this day, I really look back to my experience at J.P. Morgan as an introduction into the professional world that really helped build -- for lack of a better term -- a foundation for my career and skills I can leverage as I move forward throughout my career."

At J.P. Morgan, Duchak first worked on the business management team, providing analytics and reporting to the sales department to help build new business initiatives. He eventually transitioned to J.P. Morgan's asset management branch where he performed counterparty credit risk analysis. Although neither of these roles was strictly investing by nature, this experience proved to be an important stepping stone for Duchak's move to institutional investing. "The stuff you learn in university is not always the most applicable for the real world. Getting the exposure to different sides of the business really opened my eyes to the real world. I think the second role in counterparty credit risk really sparked the interest for investing; understanding diligence and credit analysis; analyzing balance sheets and financial statements; and really getting a sense for how to develop those skills," he said.

Duchak sees a nonprofit foundation like Kaiser as a perfect place to combine his financial skills and his interest in making a positive social impact. "I think there's a certain allure to knowing that I'm working for a place that is providing good for the American people, as opposed to just looking to make financial gains. We always like to joke here at Kaiser Family Foundation that we like to make as much money as we can, so we can give it away," he said.

David Erickson had been a derivative trader for 10 years at several investment banks on the East Coast until he started a family and moved to Madison, Wisconsin. Realizing that Madison was not where derivative-focused jobs are abundant, he found a home where he could apply investment skills, but leave the investment banking lifestyle: The University of Wisconsin Foundation.

Erickson joined the university in 2002 as an analyst. In the following eight years, he worked his way up to chief investment officer and grew the endowment's total assets from $1.2 billion to $2.4 billion. In 2009, Erickson left the university to be the chief investment officer of Ascension Investment Management, which manages the assets of Ascension Health, a health care subsidiary of Ascension, the largest nonprofit health system in the United States and the largest Catholic health system in the world.

"There are a lot of similarities between derivatives trading and institutional investing," Erickson said. In his trader days, he accumulated experience and knowledge on multiple asset classes, which helped him transition into the university endowment world. "We mostly traded in fixed-income and equity derivatives, but credit derivatives were also starting to come into play. It was a multi-asset class discussion," he said. "I like thinking about markets; you're always trying to think about if equity is going up or down, where interest rates are going to go, or whether you should do interest rate swaps or not. So when I interviewed for the position at the University of Wisconsin, there were a lot of topics that I could talk about."

In his case, another factor that helped the transition was timing. "Derivatives were being used more in institutional portfolios at that time. So, having a background in derivatives was helpful in considering whether to hedge exposure or not. The idea of synthetic exposure was starting to become more and more in favor. That was a differentiator for me in my career at the University of Wisconsin as we started to think about those things, rather than just hiring managers," he said.

Erickson's colleague at Ascension, Dale Hunt, managing director of private equity, has a similar career path of transitioning from investment banking to endowment investing and finally to health care investing.

Hunt began her career on Wall Street in 1978. She worked at the investment banking divisions of S.G. Warburg, Prudential Securities and Smith Barney. For most of her career, she focused on private market investments. In 2003, through one of her former Wall Street colleagues who later became the chief investment officer of the West Virginia University Foundation, she was offered an opportunity to join the university. "It was right after 9/11, and so I thought, 'This is maybe a good time for a change,'" Hunt said.

She went on to lead the West Virginia University Foundation's alternative investments and eventually took over as chief investment officer. At the time, Erickson was the chief investment officer of University of Wisconsin Foundation. They met as endowment chiefs, and later through this relationship, Hunt landed the position at Ascension in April 2010.

Jon Grabel spent 13 years at Baker Capital, a New York-based private equity firm, before transitioning to a public pension. Baker Capital specialized in technology, media and telecom investing. There, Grabel witnessed firsthand the ups and downs of the tech world in the early 2000s. "Being at Baker during several market cycles and seeing the height of the internet bubble to the depths of the great financial crisis, was truly illustrative in terms of how to invest, what works in different environments and how to identify patterns," he said. "I learned that investing is the easiest business in the world, until you lose money. Hopefully you learn not to make the same mistakes over again, and then you truly have the opportunity to become a good investor."

In 2014, Grabel joined the Public Employees Retirement Association of New Mexico as chief investment officer. "It is really easy to be a chief investment officer in an up-market environment. It is in a down market like this where I earn my keep, because our members need a steady hand at the tiller," he said.

For investors at institutional investment offices, public pensions might not offer the highest-paying job, but Grabel found meaning that's bigger than mere monetary gain. "I wanted to take the great experiences I had working in New York with some of the brightest, most successful people I ever come across, and apply that knowledge in a way that would have a bigger impact. Working in public pensions is potentially one of the most impactful ways that somebody can direct their career," he said.

Yup Kim, senior portfolio manager at Alaska Permanent Fund Corporation, began his career in credit investing with Silver Point Capital, a Greenwich, Connecticut-based hedge fund. Kim said this experience conditioned him to "be risk averse" and to constantly ask the question: "What could go wrong?"

"Capital preservation remains the most important lesson, and it is critical to every decision I make. The market plunge of 2007-2009 reminds me of stress-testing each opportunity against a recession or a prolonged risk-off climate, which is becoming increasingly relevant in today's environment," Kim said.

Perhaps a bigger benefit of former asset management experience, other than insights on asset classes or manager due diligence, is the professional network it helps foster. In 2011, Robert C. Lee joined the Employees' Retirement System (ERS) of Texas as director of hedge funds. Previously, he was with HFR Asset Management, a hedge fund research and management firm. "When I came here to ERS, I brought with me an understanding of the hedge fund industry's ins and outs. It's more relationship-driven than a lot of people realize. So, just being in the industry can provide you with a lot of valuable information," he said.

Another professional area where we found many institutional investors started out is -- perhaps not surprisingly -- investment consulting. Investment consultants work in the middle ground between LPs and GPs, and the job requires one to build a broad spectrum of knowledge and expertise on both sides. Therefore, it is common to see consultants transition to asset allocator and manager roles.

Rodney Overcash was a consultant to investors before he became one himself. Overcash was a researcher at firm Marquette Associates from 2001 to 2008. During his consulting days, his focus areas included asset allocation and broad portfolio construction, particularly emerging asset classes. This background gave him an edge over his peers when he joined the North Carolina Pension Fund in

2008 as an investment director. He created two new asset classes for the pension fund – credit alternatives and inflation strategies.

"[My consulting experience] provided an underlying research background as well as an understanding of how pieces of the portfolio puzzle fit together…The research background helped develop the strategic case for creating those two new asset classes," he said.

Portfolio construction is a central piece of Overcash's investment philosophy. He believes the key to make a successful portfolio is asset allocation, rather than relying solely on manager performance. He illustrated his point with the football metaphor. "There are a lot of great investment managers and a lot of great funds out there. But the fun part is how they fit together. Everybody can't be the quarterback and the running back and the wide receiver. You need some anchors on the offensive line to protect the quarterback, effectively building a team of how you want to construct a portfolio. Those types of different perspectives and experiences have influenced me to focus on how things fit together as opposed to trying to find the manager that's always trying to do the best in all different markets, which usually doesn't work out too well," he said.

After North Carolina, Overcash joined Margaret A. Cargill Philanthropies, a $9 billion private charitable foundation based in Minnesota, in 2012 as an investment director of credit strategies.

Erik Carleton, director of pension investments at Textron Inc., an industrial conglomerate with $13.4 billion in annual revenue, was an investment consultant before joining Textron in 2014. Carleton worked for NEPC, a Boston-based investment consulting firm advising more than 300 clients. "I really liked investment consulting. I had exposure to many different types of portfolios, pools of capital, investors and committees," Carleton said.

He first worked with Textron as the its external investment consultant, when the company outsourced its investment operations. Textron set up an internal investment staff in 2014 and moved all investment capabilities in house. Having a strong working relationship with Textron's chief investment officer and familiarity of the company's investment portfolio, Carleton was the top candidate when a position opened up.

"There would be two things about it that I have learned in retrospect," Carleton said. "One was the difference between advising an asset and owning an asset. On the plan sponsor side, I'm glad to be able to think of something, run it by the superiors and then actually implement it. So, you can get from advice to action. Secondly, with multiple consulting clients, anytime there was a news story, I would think 'Oh, that's terrible for this portfolio,' but then I'd think 'but that's great for this other portfolio.' Essentially, I could see how anything could ripple through different investment portfolios. Now having only one portfolio, I have a much clearer view on what I want from the markets and how I want us to be positioned."

Consultants and asset managers work with multiple clients across a broad range of portfolios and strategies. Moving to the LP side is like switching from a horizontal perspective to a vertical one, allowing one to focus on one portfolio and build strong ties with the organization. "I was an institutional consultant covering many clients with different portfolios and different objectives. I found myself wanting to dig more deeply into the investments. The opportunity to concentrate on one portfolio and focus more closely on the underlying strategies really appealed to me," said Colin Ambrose, the first chief investment officer of The Juilliard School and now the chief investment officer of UJA-Federation Of New York (United Jewish Appeal - Federation of Jewish Philanthropies of New York, Inc). Ambrose began his career at UBS Paine Webber's Asset Management and later joined his alma mater Wesleyan College to manage the endowment's alternative investments.

Ambrose's motivation to work for university endowments goes beyond just monetary reward. "The ability to give back to Wesleyan made it a great fit for me personally," he said. "Working at an endowment is an enormously gratifying experience. You get to satisfy your intellectual curiosity for evaluating interesting investment opportunities, while investing and meeting with the best investors in the world. It is personally rewarding to know that the institution you work for is using the endowment to help people in need and make the world a better place."

Public accountants, in both accounting firms and corporate offices, are another profession where many institutional investors start their careers. Similar to consultants, accountants gather knowledge and experience about institutional investing through working with institutional clients, often developing a network of investment professionals over time and transitioning into the investment side when the opportunity comes along.

Mark Rich holds a bachelor's degree and master's degree, both in accounting from Abilene Christian University. He spent his first five career years as an auditor at Ernst & Young and has won multiple industry awards, including the AICPA Young CPA of the Year Award in 2014. When he joined Kimbell Art Foundation, a Fort Worth, Texas-based private foundation, as an accountant, he didn't antic-ipate the job to be wildly different than his previous one. Yet, as he started out in the foundation's accounting function, he gradually got involved in managing the foundation's $385 million investment portfolio. This eventually led to a more profound career change.

Within two years at Kimbell, Rich earned the Certified Financial Analyst designation and increasingly shifted his focus to the investment side. "I started out working about 50/50 in accounting and finance at the foundation, but now I'm closer to 80/20 finance heavy versus the accounting. I didn't necessarily look for an investment career, but now that I found it, I really enjoy the work I do and certainly that it's with a foundation that's looking to contribute to the betterment of society," he said.

Rich said starting in public accounting gave him a solid understanding of business in general, and his auditing experience in certain sectors provides spe-cial insights on investments. "I primarily audited public oil and gas companies and that gave me a very deep knowledge in the oil and gas space, which is very beneficial to the portfolio here at the Kimbell Art Foundation, as well as under-standing investment in public companies. Seeing it from the accounting side is a very informative first-hand experience.

The audit background allowed me to take that inquisitive mind of 'Why are we doing this? Why don't we look at this investment from this perspective?' to the foundation. The audit background forces you to ask a lot of questions," he said.

Unconventional Career Path

Outside of the more traditional career paths -- investment banking, account-ing and asset management -- a number of investors hail from more tangential origins. From lawyers to real estate agents to clinical researchers, these experi-ences, more often than not, exert a large influence in shaping one's investment philosophy. "It's good to have non-investment experience in advance of building a career in finance. I believe developing a broad perspective can give a person an edge when evaluating investment opportunities," Dale Hunt of Ascension Invest-ment Management said.

Kathleen Browne, managing director at Wellesley College Investment Of-fice, has had a winding, yet interesting career path. She holds a bachelor's degree in electrical engineering from Union College and went on to attend law school in

Boston College. After earning her J.D. in 1993, Browne practiced business law for 10 years. She represented companies in private mergers and acquisitions and startup financing cases, where she worked with growth fund managers and venture capitalists. One of her long-time clients was Alcatel-Lucent Investment Management Corp., the firm that manages the Lucent corporate (today Nokia) pension fund. Browne developed a close relationship with the firm's private equity team, which at one point led to a discussion of how they could work together beyond a legal capacity. When a position opened up one year later, Browne joined the team as a private equity investor.

"Once I started working on the investment side, I felt that I had found a position that fit my talents and personality," she said.

Changing professions from engineering to law and subsequently to investing may sound like a far fetch, but Browne sees the connection among these fields. "I think the skills I developed built on each other – particularly with a start in private equity, which is so transactional and relationship-based," she said. "Engineering and law are very analytical fields. In legal practice, you also build communication skills; you learn how to listen, gather and interpret information and build trust and confidence with your clients. The skills I developed in those prior roles were very relevant for institutional investing."

Geeta Kapadia, senior investment strategist at Yale New Haven Health System's $2 billion investment office, started out working in cancer research on phase-one chemotherapy studies at the University of Chicago Hospitals. "I enjoyed working in the health care setting, but as I thought about longer-term plans, I wanted to use my educational background more, which was focused on math," she said.

Kapadia went on to work as a consultant for a Chicago-based investment advisory firm called Stratford Advisory Group (now Pavilion Advisory Group), where she got to know a network of heath care clients, and eventually led her to a position at a hospital investment office.

Having dreamt of being a physician as a child, Kapadia spent the majority of her career working in different aspects of health care across research, consulting and now investment. "I'm very happy with my position in health care. I think if I was able to have a second career, I would probably try to work in the medical field in some capacity," she said.

Jude Perez was a land associate for KB Home, a property development company, before joining the New Mexico Public Employees Retirement Association.

One responsibility of the land associate's job is producing financial models – cash flow models, for instance – for negotiations with land sellers. When one of Perez's co-workers at the KB Home left to lead a private equity portfolio for the New Mexico pension fund, Perez was offered to join. "I kind of just stumbled into the pension investing world," he said. Perez joined the pension fund in June 2010 to manage the private equity portfolio and was promoted to deputy chief investment officer in 2015.

Anthony Breault was an officer in the U.S. Navy for eight years before he joined real estate investment management firm LaSalle Partners (now Jones Lang LaSalle) through a management training program in 1997. Breault focused on leasing and management at LaSalle for eight years before transitioning to Schnitzer West, a Seattle-based property management firm to pursue real estate asset management. In 2006, he joined the Oregon State Treasury as an investment officer on the real estate team. "Jobs like this don't always come along," Breault said.

"While I really had no intentions of working in the public sector again after my military service, I was fortunate enough to be introduced to the prior CIO of the Oregon pension plan. I found him, his team and the job scope very intriguing. I had also lived overseas both in the military and while working with LaSalle. So one of my long-term goals was to gain more international experience. The opportunity to manage a large and diverse portfolio with a global reach, as well as interface with some of the best and brightest investors on the planet, sounded like a very intriguing and fantastic opportunity," he said.

2. Women In Institutional Investing

Gender balance (or lack thereof) is an enduring challenge in the traditionally male-dominated investment industry. Of the 25 women included in this book, many discussed the lack of representation of women throughout the industry, how the status of gender inequality in finance changed over time, what the industry is doing to address the issue currently and what remains to be done. While most agreed that women face unique social and professional challenges in the workplace that remain largely unaddressed, many argued that the cause is unrelated to intentional biases.

Slow Progress

Representation of women in institutional investing is growing, but progress is slow. Ample research has shown that women are as intellectually competitive as men in school and the workplace. Given the amount high-achieving women, why do so few end up in investment offices?

The answer is mixed. Some argue that the lack of representation is simply a result of less women wanting the job. "There are just fewer women who have chosen this career field," said Jennifer Wenzel, real estate investment manager at the Teacher Retirement System of Texas.

Women who defy the stereotype of a male investor are an interesting group to study. They are the driving force in shaping a more diverse and inclusive investing ecosystem and set career examples for generations of women to come. Many of them have unique stories to tell.

Betty Tse is the chief investment officer of Alameda County Employees Retirement Association in California where she leads a team of 10 investment professionals to manage the pension system's $6.9 billion of investment assets. Tse joined the association in 1999 as an investment analyst. At the time, she was the only woman in all the investment officer meetings of the State Association of County Retirement Systems -- the 20 county pension systems that are governed by California's County Employees Retirement Law of 1937.

When she became Alameda's first CIO in 2002, she would still be the only woman in all the meetings and conferences she went to. Today, she is one of the three women in SACRS.

"I'm a little surprised by the pace of the progress. 17 years later, only two more women. And, the third one just started a couple of years ago," she said in an April 2016 interview.

Tse said the slow progress is even more troublesome considering that public pensions are gender-neutral employers, meaning men and women should be treated equally in the hiring process. She observed that the talent pool was inherently out of balance because society expects women to be family caregivers first and career stars second. "Raising a family while successfully managing an institutional pension fund is one of the top difficulties facing women in the business," she said. "Family formation matters to individuals significantly. Many women decide to make the personal choice of staying at home. As a result, the talent pool would not be as big as that for the male counterpart."

Tse has been working in public funds for 17 years, 14 years as Alameda's CIO, a job that requires a lot of time and extensive travel. She said she couldn't have made it without support from her family and community, including the Alameda pension board.

The barrier to entry may go back further in history and tradition. "Women got a late start into finance. I believe many tend to go down a career path that they have been exposed to in some way, whether it's a family member's career or reading about it," said Megan Loehner, director of investments for the Missouri Local Government Employees Retirement System. "50 years ago, there were fewer women in the workforce; and of those women, there were proportionally fewer in the finance industry than, say, in nursing. Consequently, women have less exposure to the finance industry than other females who they may follow. This, combined with a lesser knowledge of the pension industry in general, causes an awareness issue."

"Over the years I think I've met with fewer, not more, women in the industry. When I graduated from college, I believed that times had changed and women would move into leadership roles in finance. Expectations were high, but the investing landscape changed. The rise of hedge funds with male-dominated, aggressive cultures, shorter-term horizons and, to some extent, greed led to less inclusion of women, which is too bad," said Mary Cahill, chief investment officer of Emory University.

Megan Loehner entered the public pension industry in 2007. Her experience echoes the same issue. "There is definitely an awareness issue in the financial industry, but especially the pension industry," she said. Loehner has a bachelor's degree and a master's degree, both in accounting. She started out as a private equity portfolio manager at the Teacher's Retirement System of Missouri. Currently she is a director of investments at the Missouri Local Government Employees Retirement System overseeing on all aspects of portfolio management.

Lela Prodani, senior investment analyst at Mercy Health, a Midwest-focused Catholic health care system with a total investment pool of $2.5 billion, began her investment career as an equity trader at a small brokerage firm called Smith, Moore & Co. She recalled that at the time the majority of financial advisors were men. The back offices usually had more women, but all the trading events she attended were "significantly dominated by men."

While today women remain a minority in the investment industry, Prodani is optimistic and confident about women working their way through organizational ranks. "I don't think gender is deterrent for success. Discrimination might have been more prevalent a long time ago, but I don't think this is really an issue anymore. I believe any woman who goes into the investment industry to succeed can do so, as long as they have the drive and passion for it," she said.

Raising Awareness

Investing is a high-pressure job that often requires extensive travel and long hours. For many qualified women investors, being in the industry is a balancing act between meeting social expectations and fulfilling professional goals.

In many cases, women not only face higher barriers of entry, but are challenged by higher hurdles climbing up the career ladder. Geeta Kapadia, senior investment strategist at Yale New Haven Health System, observed that "although quite a number of women are actually investors, unfortunately there are not as many women in decision-making positions, such as heading up investment management firms, sitting on boards, holding positions such as chief investment officer or CEO," she said.

Elaine Orr, former director of investments at Silicon Valley Community Foundation, warned that it's easy to slip into routine and accept the dynamic as a given. "I'm a minority woman who has worked in investment management for the past 20 years. When I enter a meeting, it's almost always the same audience or participants -- Caucasian men. One actually gets used to it, and I forget that I'm the only woman in the room," she said.

Orr said the leadership culture is key to promoting the inclusion of women in investment offices. "Does your senior leadership back this? That's critical for change to happen...It's proven that nimble and diverse ideas can find alpha," she said.

Amy Jensen, investment director at Northwest Area Foundation, made an interesting observation that endowments and foundations seem to house more women investors than other types of institutions. "I'm not entirely certain why that is. Maybe the women who are in senior positions at those institutions do a better job of hiring and encouraging other women. Maybe it is the presence of successful female CIOs as role models," she said.

Indeed, role models and mentors play an essential role in fostering the next generation of women investors. Many of whom we spoke to participate in efforts outside regular work that help young women embrace such careers as theirs.

Kapadia spends time volunteering for the "Women In Investment Management Initiative" launched by the CFA Institute. "It's encouraging to see such a strong participant in the market highlighting this issue," she said. Since inception, the initiative has worked with universities, fresh graduates and junior-level women investors through mentorship programs to help young women start their investing careers.

The CFA Institute is leading such initiatives across different regions in the country. Lela Prodani of Mercy Health -- located near St. Louis, Missouri -- said the CFA Society in St. Louis is organizing various events to encourage women to join the investment profession and pursue the CFA Charter, ranging from educational talks to social events. These events can be as specific as golf lessons for women. "I feel like whenever I talk to women, there are not too many females that play golf. Whenever there's a business event that involves golfing, very few women want to go," Prodani said.

One item on the St. Louis CFA Society's agenda is organizing golf outings, where instructors teach the basics and etiquette of golfing before the actual play. "This could help more women participate in business events that they otherwise wouldn't do just because they don't know how to golf," Prodani said. "I think we should also gear these events toward college students to get them educated and excited about pursuing careers in investing."

Besides professional associations like the CFA Institute, business schools and industry organizations are also channels for raising awareness. Jennifer Wenzel of Teacher Retirement System of Texas said, "I think business schools do a fairly good job of trying to encourage more women to get into the industry, but they can always innovate and improve to find new ways to encourage women to consider finance as an option." Wenzel participates in an effort called the Women's Initiative, sponsored by the Urban Land Institute, a nonprofit education and research organization focusing on the real estate industry.

Kathleen Vogelsang, chief investment officer of Grand Rapids, Michigan-based Van Andel Institute, engages in a local nonprofit organization called Michigan Women's Commission. One of the organization's core missions is promoting female engagement in STEM (science, technology, engineering and math) fields and finance. "I think we have to work at getting women interested in the math and the sciences at a young age. One of the things I hear a lot is that there just aren't a lot of women pursuing those fields. I heard that they're not promoted to higher levels because they are not visibly seen in those fields. I'd like to see a real effort in promoting women, especially those in finance. I've talked to the local universities, and they're not seeing a lot of women going into the finance majors. I think we should encourage women to do that," Vogelsang said.

Megan Loehner said women should not view each other as competitors. "Being a woman isn't our best attribute, it's being a good investor. You need to focus on expanding your skills, and that's really what will get you to be where you want to be," she said.

Equally important is supporting young women through their careers, especially at life and career crossroads. "I always wanted to work in investments, and I have always wanted to do investment analysis. There have been times in my career where people, especially men, have tried to steer me into other things, operations or client-facing roles," Amy Jensen said. "I knew what I wanted to do, and I continued to work toward that goal. I didn't let an opportunity change what I knew in my heart was what I really wanted to do and that was investing. If you know what you want to do, don't be derailed by advice, however well-meaning, that you should change your course."

Some interviewees point out that the best way to combat gender discrimination is, instead of bringing attention to the problem, focusing on the work. Ana Marshall, chief investment officer of the William and Flora Hewlett Foundation, said gender discrimination was never an issue in her 20-year career in institutional investing. "It's always been about, 'can you deliver?' Luckily, unlike other industries, this is a numbers industry. You are as good as your numbers. As long as your numbers are good, you are willing to work really long hours and travel frequently, there is opportunity," she said.

Due to the high-pressure of the job, especially at the chief investment officer and senior investment professional levels, Marshall said many women -- and men -- self-select themselves out from senior-level roles. "These are jobs with a great deal of responsibility, and for both men and women, it's hard to stay balanced. I would say CIOs and senior asset class directors have more balance than investment banking, but our spouses would probably disagree there is balance in our lives. We are on planes all the time. We miss our kids' birthdays and recitals. We miss our anniversaries. We have the same trade-offs as men in these roles."

However, that doesn't mean the issue and perception of sexism doesn't exist. "I have heard from a few of my peers that there is an unspoken boys network that could at times undermine the chief investment officer," Marshall said. While some people may see it as a sexism issue at workplace, Marshall takes a more objective perspective. "That sounds like something that could be related to how a specific board functions and less about the woman in the job. Board delegation is usually an investment policy issue, and it's written regardless of whether the CIO is female or a male. It's simply conflicts arise in moments of high stress. For example, during the crisis, some people felt that is was a sexist thing when a board questions you. I would say it wasn't. It was about how you are doing, how the portfolio returns look, and your relationship with the board," she said.

To address the "boy network" issue at the governance level, Marshall advocates for more inclusion of women on the board. "That's a long-term plan. I'm starting to see more openness to having women at the board level," she said.

3. Lessons Learned

Institutional investing can be exhausting, demanding and tedious at times. To excel, not only does it require hard credentials but qualities and skills that aren't easily enumerated on paper. We asked many of our interviewees what their best career lessons are and what advice they would give to the aspiring institutional investors. A few repeated themes include mentorship, team spirit, constant self-improvement and, the most important, an insatiable passion for the job.

Network, Network, Network

"Institutional investing is a people business and emotional intelligence is essential," said Yup Kim of Alaska Permanent Fund.

As noted in previous sections of this chapter, it's common for people to have similar work histories. And at some point past entry level, job changes are often spurred by recommendations and referrals from former colleagues and friends. Chris Halaska, a former investment banker at JPMorgan, cultivated a broad network of CEOs and CFOs at health care systems when he worked on capital raising, strategic engagements and mergers and acquisitions for the industry. One of his clients was the CFO of Memorial Hermann Health System, the largest nonprofit health care system in Texas. Knowing that Halaska had 12 years of investment experience, he offered Halaska a position leading the hospital system's treasury function. Halaska joined Memorial Hermann in 2012 as the senior vice president and chief investment officer, managing the hospital system's $3 billion investment assets.

The benefit of having a strong professional network extend beyond landing a senior-level job to honing investment skills, namely meeting, vetting and hiring external asset managers.

Dean Duchak, director of investments at Kaiser Family Foundation, hardly knew anyone in San Francisco when his firm relocated from New York to the West Coast. He had to break into the finance community there from ground zero. "It was challenging," he said, "[but] it was one that I welcomed very much, because it really forced me to build these relationships that I now have."

Building a network and fostering new relationships can take months, often years, but the benefits are self-evident, especially for investors who must operate in a global setting. As Duchak discovered, the San Francisco finance circle was "an eclectic but tight-knit group of people."

"There are folks that I've come to call friends as much as I'd call colleagues or industry peers," he said. "I think it's been a wonderful experience to do that, and not necessarily have that same group of people that I've known forever who I would normally just associate with otherwise."

Team Spirit vs. Independent Thinking

American culture is known for its individualism, and people are cautious getting caught up in groupthink. However, interviewees strongly believe in the power of collaboration. Jed Johnson, senior managing director at Crow Holdings Capital - Investment Partners, a $2 billion multi-family office, views career improvement in two parts: "working in the business" and "working on the business." "One of the things I've tried to be consistent about in my own career is always looking for ways to do what we do better. We all are required to come to work every day and do our jobs to the very best of our ability – that is 'working in our business.' At the same time, we should also always think about how we can improve what we're doing – that is 'working on our business.'" he said. "They are two different things, and I think keeping in mind that working on your business is as important as working in your business is probably the best recommendation I would give to anyone about trying to build success in any career."

"If you keep things very focused on the mission of the institution that you are supporting, then the job is not just a job -- it's a passion," said Mauricia Geissler, chief investment officer at Amherst College. "I think you have to be connected or believe in the mission of the institution that you work for. That just makes it that much more exciting. There's good and bad with every job, but it makes the bad days not seem so bad!"

That said, in an investor's day-to-day job, nothing is more imperative than being able to think independently and having a clear understanding of oneself, as stressed by many investors we spoke to. This applies to new industry entrants and senior-level investors alike.

"It's really about knowing yourself -- what you're good at, what drives you and what you enjoy," Ron Virtue of JM Family Enterprises said.

"I find it very disappointing when candidates haven't done a true self-assessment and are not self-aware," Elaine Orr, former investment director of Silicon Valley Community Foundation, spoke of a frequent frustration she encounters while hiring for the nonprofit she led. "You should ask yourself, 'What are my motivators?' And also, 'What are the strengths I'm bringing to the table?'"

Mary Cahill of Emory University believes defending one's own voice is particularly important for women. "My advice is be vocal," she said. "This is a great industry, and there should be more women in investment management. Networking is important, especially in the very early part of one's career or during times of volatility. People should be themselves, not try to be someone else."

Indeed, the advice applies to all investors regardless of gender, especially at organizations with a culture of hierarchies. Jude Perez of New Mexico PERA said, "I think the one thing about working for a public fund or a pension is that the organizations are very hierarchical. Sometimes junior professionals don't speak up as much as they should because of this."

Many chief investment officers we interviewed emphasized the value of staying focused in their job, which can be difficult, as chief investment officers need to make decisions for various aspects of the investment portfolio while managing a relationship with the organization's' leadership team such as investment boards or committees.

Sam Masoudi, chief investment officer of the Wyoming Retirement System, said trying to make everyone happy will only make you a myopic investor. "If you worry too much about keeping people happy in the short term, you end up becoming a short-term investor; you will end up following the herd and producing poor returns," he said. "Focus on long-term returns. It will increase the chances of producing superior returns and keeping your board happy."

Lawrence Kochard, chief investment officer of the University Of Virginia Investment Management Company, said "being able to get the right lessons from best-in-class without getting sucked into being part of a herd" is challenging. "You need to be in constant learning mode and assume that there's something you can learn from anyone in the business."

Some of our interviewees offered more specific advice for one to pull off a senior-level job. "Find a way to get a broad base of experiences early on, rather than just focusing on one area. If you want to be a chief investment officer, you need to know something about all the asset classes," said Erik Lundberg, chief investment officer of the University of Michigan. Lundberg's investment office has a multi-year rotational program for entry-level analysts, in which they were placed on different teams divided by asset class before they work on any specific area. "They get a broad base of experiences. Later, when they end up having to focus most of their time on one asset class, they also have an ability to relate to what's going on in all other asset classes," Lundberg said.

Colin Ambrose of UJA-Federation Of New York said chief investment officers should also keep an eye open for low-probability events. "It's not the probability of the disastrous event occurring, but the consequences of it occurring. You need to ask yourself, 'If this low-probability event happens, can our institution live with the negative outcome?' If the answer is no, then don't invest. You owe it to your institution to always live to fight another day," he said.

Don't Quit Reading

A number of interviewees mentioned they keep the habit of reading, whether it's investments-related or not, to better themselves as investors. "Be a voracious reader," Yup Kim of Alaska Permanent Fund said. "Investing well goes beyond understanding financial theory and following markets. Equally important is understanding geopolitics, legal and judicial frameworks, economic history, demographic trends, human psychology, biological sciences, disruptive technologies, big picture themes and connecting all the dots."

David Erickson of Ascension Investment Management recommended a book he's currently reading, *Antifragile: Things That Gain From Disorder* by Nassim Nicholas Taleb, a philosophical essay collection that has little to do with investments, but Erickson said would benefit investors. "The book talks about how if you're a fragile person or industry as you go through volatility, it makes you weaker. If you're an antifragile person or industry and you go through volatility, it makes you stronger. I think that on the investment side, you have to be ready to go through up periods and down periods. You're never always going to be right. If you're able to develop a team, a psyche and a process, then having that mindset with your group as you go through volatility doesn't shake your conviction, it actually makes you stronger," he said.

"In hindsight, 2008 and 2009 were really rough periods to go through, and I think the lessons I learned then made me a better investor. So, I would recommend reading that book and then discussing it with someone who has gone through volatility on the job to get an understanding of that. You're going to go through volatility in your career, and managing that while also making yourself stronger is important," he said.

Sean Feng of Kresge Foundation said he reads extensively as a way to form his investment philosophy. A research scientist-turned investor, he started learning about the industry by diligently listening to NPR's The Marketplace and reading the Wall Street Journal. "Discover and internalize some core tenets of long-term investing through reading books," he advised junior investors who aspire to enter the industry. Feng's top recommendation is to read the Berkshire Hathaway annual letters. "If you have time, go back and try to read all of them," he said.

Another investment book for entry-level investors is *The Most Important Thing: Uncommon Sense for The Thoughtful Investor* by Howard Marks, recommended by Scott Davis, chief investment officer of the Indiana Public Retirement System.

Market conditions constantly change, and investing is an ongoing learning process. Dean Duchak of Kaiser Family Foundation said, "You spend the first three-to-five years learning 80 percent of what institutional investment or foundation investing is about in terms of asset allocation, due diligence and whatnot. Then you spend the rest of your career trying to chase down that final 20 percent. You might not ever get there, and that's a good thing; that means you're constantly challenging yourself and growing as an investor."

Part II

INVESTMENT TEAM

In the years leading up to 2012, Illinois Municipal Retirement Fund's investment office had a relatively flat hierarchy. Much of the staff had the same title, investment analyst, and reported to a superior, an investment manager.

When Dhvani Shah was named chief investment officer in December 2011, she reshaped the team to create layers of authority and a ladder on which junior employees could work into senior roles. "The department is structured such that there is opportunity for growth and advancement," Shah said. "An associate analyst can move up two levels under the existing structure. By creating that growth opportunity, you can attract and retain staff."

Today, a fully staffed investment team consists of 14 individuals organized by five key function areas: private markets, public markets, emerging managers, total portfolio and operations.

Shah's structure is representative of the path many institutions have taken to manage complex multi-billion-dollar portfolios: a nimble team; organized to match the investment thesis; a degree of specialization in the senior ranks but a tendency toward collaborative generalism; and the opportunity for career advancement -- a key in retaining talent.

4. Nimbleness, A Necessity

Investment teams come in all shapes and sizes. They have varying invest-ment strategies and near-term liabilities. However, whether a young single-family office or a monolithic pension fund, a natural proclivity for being nimble and adapting to the resource constraints of the institution is a strong current that ties all investment offices -- perhaps all places of employment.

Amy Jensen of Northwest Area Foundation is an extreme of this ideal. She is the sole investment professional managing $420 million across public, private and mission-related investments at the foundation. A team of one is not uncom-mon for a portfolio of that size, she noted. "In addition to trying to meet our return requirements, which for a private foundation with no capital inflows and a perpetual time horizon is obviously difficult, we're also trying to have a positive social impact," Jensen said.

When Jensen was offered access to a fund at the end of 2014, she was torn. It was the end of the year and the due diligence would have to be completed in a compressed timeframe of just a few weeks. "It was at the end of the year, which is a very busy time, and I wasn't sure it was worth dropping everything else to get it done," she said.

So Jensen relied on her network to vet the opportunity. For as much as the investment world is predicated on hard metrics like return multiples and fee struc-tures, many deals are made based on the quality of lead investors and other limited partners. Piggybacking on another team's due diligence is an efficient means to determining the base viability of the opportunity.

She consulted the investment team at Carleton College, which had already committed capital to the fund. After that conversation, she was swayed.

"...They knew the team well and convinced me that it was worth the effort it would take to get it done in a tight time frame," she said. "We are all resource constrained, and one way to deal with that is to cultivate strong relationships with your peers and share everything that you can."

This concept is not, however, relegated to extremes. Yup Kim is on a five-per-son private markets team at the Alaska Permanent Fund Corporation, a $55 billion sovereign wealth fund. As senior portfolio manager, Kim is in charge of the spe-cial opportunities subset of the private markets allocation.

The private markets team is mandated with adding uncorrelated alpha to the broader portfolio through private equity, special opportunities, infrastructure, private credit and absolute return investments.

"Given our small team, we're required to wear many hats," Kim said. "Our private equity mandate requires us to be specialists, while the special opportunities mandate requires us to be nimble generalists."

Bill Camelio is part of a three-person team managing $2 billion in assets for the Yale-New Haven hospital system. While the team is split along asset class lines, there is collaboration and consensus on investment decisions.

"[Being in charge of the absolute return and global fixed income allocations] does not mean my colleagues are not involved in the process or that I do not get involved in other areas of the portfolio," Camelio said. "Because we are a small team, it's usually all hands on deck when it comes to making changes."

Since joining Yale-New Haven in 2014, the team has sought diversification into new asset classes and investment opportunities, despite their limited resources.

"We have explored investing in unconstrained fixed income, we moved from hedge fund of funds into direct hedge fund relationships, and recently made changes on our developed international equity portfolio," Camelio said. "We have attacked all of these initiatives as a team."

"We are a team of four and have a flexible mandate allows us to react to these things," Dean Duchak, director of investments at the Kaiser Family Foundation said. "We try to consistently hammer home that we need to be long-term focused. Short-term volatility is a very tough thing for a lot of managers, but volatility should create opportunity. If we have the ability to look a bit further on down the road and remain steadfast in that view, hopefully we should be able to take advantage of that volatility. But I think being a small team certainly allows us to be a little bit more nimble and flexible in the way that we do manage and make subtle changes to the portfolio."

5. Structures Of An Investment Team

There is no simple answer to how an investment team is structured. A mixture of variables -- resource constraints, the chief investment officers' philosophy of approaching markets and the institution's near-term liability -- dictate how team's are structured, resulting in a variety of unique, but related, approaches.

Asset Class

The most common means of dividing the labor is by asset class. The University of Minnesota Foundation, New Mexico Educational Retirement Board, CHRISTUS Health, Yale-New Haven Health System and Massachusetts Public Retirement Investment Management are a handful of the numerous examples of this strategy.

At the University of Minnesota Foundation, Chief Investment Officer Stuart Mason oversees a staff of five to manage the $2.2 billion endowment and $1.2 billion in a variety of other capital pools, including working capital, insurance reserves and a long-term capital savings account pool. The team ranges from a three-year analyst level position to senior portfolio managers with more than 15 years of experience.

In addition to Mason's broad portfolio management responsibilities, he is the venture capital portfolio manager. One portfolio manager oversees private equity and return-generating fixed income; two investment professionals co-manage the real assets portfolios; and a final portfolio manager is responsible for hedge funds and fixed income for both the endowment and the other pools of capital.

A keen reader will notice that Mason's team does not include a public market portfolio manager. That's because the Minnesota Foundation invests nearly 50 percent of its portfolio in private markets and leaves the public equities to index funds.

"We just don't have time or bandwidth to try to pick public stock managers, where if we succeed, we earn an extra 50-100 basis points," Mason said. "If we want to underwrite a private equity fund, we may get an extra 500 basis points or 1,000 basis points."

This is a prime example of how a chief investment officer's investment strategy directly dictates the composition of a team structure that, although delineated by asset class, is unique in its approach.

Many institutions, however, take a more macro view of labor distribution along asset class lines. Instead of breaking the portfolio into narrow buckets, these institutions operate through a lens of public markets and private markets.

When Bob Jacksha was named chief investment officer of New Mexico Educational Retirement Board in 2007, he embarked on a plan to diversify the pension plan's assets. He grew the five-person team to 11 individuals split along a public-private divide. Reporting directly to Jacksha are two deputy CIOs: one in charge of alternatives, the other managing public markets and credit.

"From that history as a small team, there was a lot of collaboration required," Jacksha said. "We still retain that dynamic today to a good degree."

Public Employees' Retirement Association of New Mexico also splits their investment team along asset class lines, but instead of traditional asset classes or a public-private view, Jonathan Grabel, chief investment officer, takes an orthogonal approach, which stems from his view of markets.

There are, Grabel said, only three asset classes: equities, fixed income and real assets. Those asset classes can then be broken down into liquid or illiquid. For further granularity, some of those categories can be collated depending on whether a mandate is long-only or long-short.

When Grabel joined the pension fund in January 2014, he restructured the team toward this logic and away from its breakdown along traditional asset class lines.

Prior to Grabel joining, the pension fund's head of equities focused on traditional long-only equities. She now oversees the entire global equity portfolio -- long-only equities, hedged equity and private equity. The same pattern is applied to the fixed income and real assets.

To ensure that the three segments not overlap or work against one another, the pension fund has an asset allocation portfolio manager to work across asset classes and facilitate knowledge sharing across the teams.

"For example, if one manager is overweight a position, another is short that same position, and we are paying active manager fees for both, then we sub-optimize at the portfolio level," Grabel said. "These are the type of pitfalls we look to avoid."

A consequence of this investment philosophy is a focus on "the predominant risk factor associated with the major asset categories, as opposed to the wrapper or vehicle in which an investment product resides."

"Fundamentally, the equity risk premium or equity beta is the main driver of equity returns," Grabel said. "The underlying portfolio construct, be it low volatility, hedge or illiquid, is a second order determinant of returns.

In essence, Grabel's approach to team construction uses risk as the defining variable for organization. The Margaret A. Cargill Philanthropies, a far newer team, relied on a similar strategy.

Rodney Overcash runs the credit sleeve at Cargill. He joined the foundation in September 2012 as part of a new investment team being assembled by the firm's chief investment officer, Shawn Wischmeier. "A more siloed model has worked and has been great for a lot of organizations," Overcash said. "We had the opportunity, because we're so new, to build a team from scratch with a completely new pool of capital and try something different. And it's working out pretty well."

Wischmeier recognized the strategy of splitting a team by public and private investments, but thought there was a better way, Overcash said.

"The way he structured was similar to a portfolio risk profile, like credit," Overcash said. "My team runs anything from long-only, fixed-income rates, investment grade credit, high-yield credit to long-short credit hedge funds to private debt opportunities, distressed and mezzanine-type debt."

Cargill has an identical team structure: an equity team, a credit team, a real assets team and a risk management and asset allocation team. Each investment professional has experience in different types of investment structures, he said, and thus they can be structure agnostic.

"If the equity team sees an opportunity in a particular space -- like health care -- would we rather play that through the public markets or is it a better opportunity for the private side or would they want to introduce a group that can go for a long-short hedge fund style?" Overcash said. "This recognizes the fact that opportunities could be missed based on public team versus private team structures. We are set up to let the teams be able to look across structures."

David Holmgren, chief investment officer at Hartford HealthCare, thinks that bringing risk management to the forefront of investment management is a fundamental change to the industry.

"A very unique idea that we are passionate about is that risk management is not meant to be a back office function, but with me in the leadership team in the front office," he said. "To us that's a very unique cultural aspect as to how we designed this investment office, whereas in other endowment offices risk management is more of watching the guardrails..."

The Washington University Investment Management Company takes a slightly different approach to team construction by viewing things through the lens of liquidity. The management company has a public liquids team, a private illiquids team and an absolute return team, which cuts across public and private markets.

Mark Newcomb is director of the public liquids, which includes liquid credits, liquid equities, liquid rates and currencies. "I think endowments, in general, are moving toward that more unconstrained, creative way that they can better deploy capital," Newcomb said. "It's like a process improvement mentality that endowments are starting to get really acute with, because it's going to be a lot more difficult environment for the next 10 years than the last 10."

Nonetheless, regardless of the opportunity, Newcomb recognizes, once again, the need for being nimble and collaborative. To foster that spirit, the Washington University moved into an open office.

"We often find that our best investment opportunities are unique and require collaboration," Newcomb said. "It may fall in one area to underwrite and invest, but might require several different points of reference or skill from other areas. So, we're growing in our collaboration."

Generalists, Specialists & The Blur Between

When it comes to structuring an investment team, there is another way of looking at organization, which fall into three distinct approaches: a pure generalist model, a pure specialist model and a blend. The distribution of models across the industry favors pure generalism at smaller institutions, with a hybrid model appearing more commonly as assets, and thus team size, increase. A purely specialist team is less common.

i. Generalist

For some institutions, specialism is an unaffordable or unnecessary luxury due to natural resource constraints. Others see it as building walls through which information sharing and learning opportunities are impermeable. Nonetheless, there is consensus that on a small team, a generalist structure naturally entails cross training the staff, a major tool for team stability and retention.

At the UJA-Federation Endowment, Colin Ambrose and his team have a generalist structure. The team has a point person for each manager but collaborates on every investment decision.

"We have dedicated weekly meetings to discuss the macro environment, our pipeline of opportunities, portfolio monitoring and our ongoing projects." Ambrose said. "This allows everyone's voice to be heard and enables us to work through our pipeline of opportunities in a disciplined manner."

"We're a small team managing a focused portfolio," he said. "We don't have a large number of manager relationships. Utilizing a generalist approach enables everybody to be intricately involved in the whole portfolio."

Amherst College has a team of six generalists led by Mauricia Geissler. The value proposition of a generalist model, Geissler says, is the ability to work across asset classes.

"You're not siloed as you might be at a bigger institution, as is the case with a lot of pension funds where you work in public equities, public fixed income or real estate," Geissler said. "I do think that's an attractive opportunity, no matter where you are in your career development."

It is important to note that while teams may be divided by asset class, it doesn't mean they are specialists. Such is the case at Amherst.

"We're a flat organization," she said. "We do everything as a team. While one person may be leading the charge in research on a particular manager or a segment of the market, it's a very collegiate environment."

The Alfred P. Sloan Foundation runs fewer line items than some of its peers, which allows it to have a concentrated team of generalists.

"If you can look across capital structures, liquidity and markets, I think you become a better investor," said Elizabeth Hewitt, chief investment officer at the Alfred P. Sloan Foundation. "At the end of the day, I think that people who do work across these areas have a great advantage in learning and becoming a well-rounded asset allocator and investor."

The same applies to Employees' Retirement System of Texas where Robert C. Lee served as director of hedge funds on a team on a team of generalists.

"Turn over a lot of rocks and kiss a lot of frogs," Lee said. "That is certainly encouraged, as well as building relationships with not only the hedge funds but other allocators who are thought-leaders within the industry. I think that ultimately helps us gain an edge in sourcing."

Scott Davis joined Indian Public Retirement System in December 2010 as director of public equity. In the years since, Davis has worked his way up the ranks and assumed the role of chief investment officer in June 2016.

"When I first started, the team had a silo mentality, and there was little collaboration amongst asset class directors/analysts to share best ideas," Davis said in an email.

In order to facilitate communication between teams, Indiana PRS opened manager meetings to every team member, began hosting team-wide education sessions and instituted analyst-only meetings.

"We have tried to construct an investment organization that is fairly flat to make sure the best ideas are escalated quickly and to get diversification in thought," Davis said. "This is an area we are continually trying to come up with creative ideas for improvement."

For Katheryn Crecelius, who retired from a decade-long tenure as chief investment officer at Johns Hopkins University in June 2016, a generalist model better adheres to the changing investment landscape.

"It was part of my vision that I wanted the team to be generalists," Crecelius said prior to her retirement. "When I came, I felt that if ever the world had been neatly compartmentalized into public equity, private equity, real estate, etc., that the boundaries of the different asset sub-classes are weakening."

Not only did Crecelius want her staff to gain a thorough understanding of every asset class and manager, but take a macro view of the portfolio.

"How do we protect ourselves against inflation?" she said, exemplifying the questions she expected her staff to consider. "How do we protect against deflation? Is real estate an inflation hedge? ...I want people to be able to engage with those big picture asset allocation questions and not simply the more silo-ed asset class questions."

Girard Miller may have summed it up best: "We are not big enough to have real specialists, said Miller, who retired as chief investment officer from Orange County's $14 billion employees' retirement system in January 2017. "Most of our meetings with money managers are with the full team so that we can cross-train in case we lose somebody, which is always a business risk in a system like ours."

Only firms of a certain size can specialize, Miller said. "It's only when you get up to the jumbo state plans that you start seeing a lot of staff specialization and in-house money management."

ii. The General-Specialist Mix

A mixed system of specialists in senior ranks and generalists in the newer positions is a very popular model. The proponents of the system argue that it best utilizes asset class experts to prudently invest and teach the younger team members.

The investment office at Memorial Sloan-Kettering is prime example of this strategy. Jason Klein, chief investment officer, established a hierarchy of senior investors who are specialized in public or private assets.

One of those specialists is Novisi Nirschl, director of private markets. She oversees venture capital, private equity, natural resources, real estate, intellectual property and opportunistic investments.

As you move down the experience spectrum, the middle- and lower-level investment professionals are generalists and work across both public and private investments.

The team as a whole is highly collaborative and meets regularly," Nirschl said. "That [structure] helps to make it less siloed within the team and more collaborative, which was intentional."

Chief Investment Officer Lawrence Kochard takes a similar approach. Working beneath Kochard, the University of Virginia Investment Management Company has six managing directors that each have a specialty, or as Kochard likes to call it, a "core expertise."

One of his managing directors, for instance, is head of long-only public equity, co-head of long-short public equity and co-head of growth equity. Another managing director is co-head of long-short and co-head of venture capital.

A unique aspect of Kochard's system is that although his senior staff has specialties, they are not purely siloed in their field of expertise.

"I've got this approach where people have a core expertise," Kochard said. "Then, over time, I want them to broaden out and become more generalist."

His strategy embodies the spirit of what Kathryn Crecelius said in the generalist section of this chapter: a desire for the team to view the portfolio holistically.

"Over time, I want everyone to really think of what are the best ideas for the fund as opposed to thinking narrowly within a certain bucket, but not completely generalist meaning they can work on anything at any point in time," he said. "I want everyone to have a core level expertise."

Below the managing directors are a layer of associates, senior analysts and analysts that are all generalists.

"They work with all the managing directors on different projects and really will have an opportunity to work on every part of the portfolio," Kochard said.

Before his retirement in June 2016, Mark Barnard spent more than 20 years managing private markets at the Howard Hughes Medical Center's investment office.

Barnard was part of a 15-member investment team where the senior staff specialized by asset class. Nonetheless, it was a collegiate environment of collaboration.

"We have an integrated investment effort," Barnard said. "So, we speak across asset classes on any particular idea or market opportunity, whether that is long-only, hedge funds, real asset or private equity. I think the integration really helps."

And then there is Dhvani Shah, who was detailed in full at the outset of this chapter. She restructured the team to create layers as well. Investors later in their career can specialize in their asset class, while newer staff work across the portfolio.

"Because we are a team of 14 investment professionals, it is just large enough to specialize in something, yet small enough that you can be part of broader projects," Shah said.

6. Team Size, Culture & Retention

All of the team structures detailed previously are predicated on the fact that the institutions can and will devote significant capital to supporting a multi-person investment office. Many endowments and foundations with less than $1 billion in assets will outsource their investment functions to third parties. For those with in-house investment staff, many are a one- or two-person operation, like Northwest Area Foundation's sole investor Amy Jensen, mentioned earlier in this chapter.

Across the industry, investment teams range in size from one individual to robust teams of more than 100. Interestingly, no matter if it's a team of six or 36, most describe their team as small. So what is the ultimate team size and what kind of culture should it have? Again, no easy answer.

Chief Investment Officer Michael Trotsky manages the $62 billion Massachusetts Pension Reserves Investment Management Board. He is the head of a specialized 16-person all-star team with multiple Ph.D. holders and many with money management experience. But his team didn't always look like this.

"During the past five years we've been really successful in rebuilding the investment team, which, in the aftermath of the world financial crisis, was really decimated," Trotsky said in a January 2016 interview. "It was down 11 employees, nine key employees, and it was the result of a compensation philosophy and plan that was constantly in flux and not well supported."

Although the pension fund has a large capital base, it is still a government entity. This meant Trotsky was unable to pay as well as Wall Street. So how did he recruit this team?

"...The work here is very, very interesting," he said. "There's a lot of responsibility. I give my direct reports a lot of autonomy."

Like many of the institutions mentioned previously, Mass PRIM is divided by traditional asset classes and has a blend of specialized senior roles and more generalised junior roles. However, like Kochard's UVIMCO team, Trotsky implemented a program in 2015 to allow high performing employees to rotate to other teams.

"That's been a thrust for us for the past year is to allow people in any one silo to contribute to other silos," Trotsky said. "This is the kind of thing that I hope, and so far so good, makes the job more interesting to people, even though I may not be able to pay them what the private sector pays."

Also important to Trotsky is providing a reasonable work-life balance. One of his directors is also a professor at Brandeis University. If he needs to leave work mid-day for class, Trotsky said, that's perfectly fine. Mass PRIM also expanded its parental leave program to 12 weeks from four weeks.

"We're trying to think of everything to make PRIM a good lifestyle choice as well," he said.

Rewarding an efficient and effective team for their hard work is a common, almost obvious, theme for attracting and retaining talent. The definition of reward could mean allotting time to teach a class, tend to a newborn baby or maybe just hanging out with the team outside of work.

Mauricia Geissler and her team at Amherst have an open office space, active dialogues and an enviable work ethic, but after that they make sure to spend quality time with one another.

"We do a lot of fun things outside the office together too," Geissler said. "When we're in the office though, we work darn hard to make sure we're doing everything we need to in order to make money for the college."

The key is not a magic number of people or a particular cocktail of benefits. It's about finding a group of individuals that work well together, respect each other's needs and care about driving the mission of the institution forward.

Megan Loehner is director of investments at the Missouri Local Government Employees Retirement System where she and the chief investment officer manage the entire $6.5 billion portfolio.

"We both work on everything, from long-term capital market assumptions to manager selection," Loehner said. "It just depends on who has the time to actually lead the process versus just being there for support. None of us are perfect. So, we try to hire others who complement us. In areas I feel I am weak, Brian is strong and vice versa."

On a small team, Loehner argues, it is all the more important that there be chemistry between coworkers.

"Because this industry is very demanding and because we have a small team, we don't have time to deal with personalities that don't fit well," she said. "We are a very transparent group, and that requires a lot of trust."

With that trust comes an ability to venture into more difficult and potentially rewarding terrains. Loehner and her boss actively pursue private market deals that might otherwise deter such a small team.

"I think it would be just as challenging for a team of 22," Loehner said. "It's challenging for anyone, in general, to actually get some kind of benchmark data to make a quantifiable decision. With a team of two, we've found a way that works for us."

For Mark Barnard, and many of the others Trusted Insight interviewed, the mission of the organization was a key driver in attracting and retaining staff.

"One of the things that incentivizes people here at Howard Hughes Medical Institute, and the investment team particularly, is our mission," he said. "It's been very successful; we have employed 25 Nobel Prize winning scientists over the long term. One of the reasons people stick around is not just the positive nature of the intellectual environment here, but because people like the mission of the institute. Everybody cares for the reputation of the institute in a really sensible and important way."

The average tenure, at the time of our interview, of Howard Hughes managing directors was roughly 15 years, according to Barnard.

"I think that continuity of talent has really made a big difference," he said. "We're collegial, and we've known each other a long time. There's a lot of mutual respect, but also rigorous discussions about how to approach any market opportunity."

The University of Michigan investment office also has long tenures at the senior level, says Chief Investment Officer Erik Lundberg. This allows Michigan to take its time to build up the investment team.

"We staff fairly traditionally, but compared to other endowments, we may have a larger portion of junior investment staff," Lundberg said. "We have a great staff of junior investment analysts who help with providing the necessary management analytics for us to manage this amount of money with a relatively small staff."

Jeremy Wolfson, chief investment officer at the $12 billion Los Angeles Water and Power Employees' Retirement Plan, compared his team to that of a firm on Wall Street. The 10-person team is broken down by two senior investment officers controlling public markets and private markets, respectively, with investment officers under their purview who are divided by asset class.

"I've tried to create a culture here that's very similar to a Wall Street culture, within the constraints that we have at the government," Wolfson said. "It's a very collegial, high-performance team."

Chris Ailman runs California State Teachers' Retirement System's colossal $178.7 billion investment office that employs more than 130 investment professionals. Ailman likened his culture to a sports team.

"A lot of cultures can lead to positive alpha, but when the culture changes, that's when the alpha disappears," Ailman said. "If you think about it, think of any sports team and when they change head coaches and change culture, their record deteriorates generally. It's common sense."

Not only is CalSTRS a consensus-driven, collegiate environment, according to Ailman, but the staff is diverse, with an even split of males and females.

"That is so unusual for Wall Street, but I am really proud of how we've built up our staff and the talent that we have," he said. "I think it's led to better decision making."

The key to keeping that culture, Ailman said, is for the whole organization to be held accountable, from senior staff to new hires.

"...Management lives it and walks the talk," Ailman said. "We don't demand the core staff to follow our culture. We actually demand management to follow the culture, and it flips it on its head but it really works here."

Constant communication and defined team roles are what Renee Hanna, director of investments at Baylor University's investment office, attributes to their team success.

"...We sit right across the hall from each other. We are not waiting for the internal committee meeting to discuss an investment," Hanna said. "We're discussing things in real time, day to day. There's a lot of discussion on marketable versus private. So, we're not operating in a silo. I think communication and teamwork is key. We all have different backgrounds, viewpoints and experiences and leverage each other to make sound investment decisions."

The six-person Baylor investment team also consists of equal parts male and female.

"...I feel very fortunate to work with a great group of male and female investment professionals," she said. "There are six people in our office, half men and half women. We have a great team with equal voice, and I attribute that to the leadership of our CIO, Brian Webb."

Kim Lew, chief investment officer of the Carnegie Corporation, emphasized the critical importance of diversity of thought, character and even geographic heritage so well that it's best to just read her words in totality.

"Diversity is such a huge part of Carnegie, and it has made a huge difference in the dialogue we have, how we engage and how we create value," Lew said in an October 2015 interview when she was serving as co-chief investment officer. "I would be remiss in not saying that we are a team that is more women than is probably typical, even in the foundation space. We have people from all over the globe, as far as where they've lived and where they grew up. The one thing that we are not sufficiently diverse in is schools. We all come from the same schools, and that's the common strategic bent that binds us. We think about things from a slightly different perspective. Some people come from a nonprofit background, a development background. Some people come from real estate. Some people come from a much more technical background. We have east coast, we have west coast, we have people from the middle. All of that makes for really healthy conversation. That's an important part of who we are."

The Weinberg Foundation's Jonathan Hook reinforced that sentiment: that institutional investment is a people business and cultural fit is paramount to success.

"You have to have good people, and there a tremendous number of good people in this business across all endowments, foundations and pensions," said Hook, the foundation's chief investment officer. "It was nice to focus on building a small team that could be very cohesive and create the culture that I felt could fit into the existing culture at the foundation."

The strategy that Kathryn Crecelius found to work during her ten-year tenure at Johns Hopkins was to build the institutional investor she wanted from the ground up.

"Endowments management is really an apprenticeship business," Crecelius said. "You can't learn to do it in school; you have to learn by doing. I prefer to grow my own team rather than going out and hiring senior investment officers."

When she joined Johns Hopkins, she hired one investment officer and kept the existing officer. Everyone else, she said, was hired as an analyst.

Onc was basically two years out of college, was working for one of the investment banks in wealth management and had started working on his CFA," she said. "So, he had gotten his feet wet in the investment business, but was really at a stage where we knew we could teach him and train him. That was the pattern that we applied to everybody else."

Carnegie Mellon University's Chief Investment Officer Charles Kennedy boiled the appeal of joining his close-knit team to an elevator pitch.

"First, there is the CMU culture – a direct, no-pretense, roll-up-your-sleeves attitude to achieve your goals with limited resources," Kennedy said. "Second, the university has top programs in several areas in technology. Investing in human innovation and entrepreneurship comes naturally, as the university's name would suggest. Last, Carnegie Mellon is a global institution. Our students and faculty come from around the world. Thinking and investing globally is key to our strategy."

Courtney Powers, director of marketable alternatives at the University of Texas Investment Management Company, describes a no-nonsense environment of healthy debate across the team.

"The entire team is expected to have an opinion on every investment and there are dissenting views at times," Powers said. "That's good. Our job is to constantly force curve the existing managers in the portfolio and we need to challenge each other's individual view. You can make a bull or bear case for any investment and having healthy, objective debate is vital if we are to make better decisions long term. What's nice is that we don't "have" to make any particular investment. If there is a significant disagreement, then the probability we put on long-term success is lower, therefore it's more likely the investment would not be made."

Part III

PORTFOLIO

An institutional investment office should be thought of as a living entity. The investment policy is the DNA of a firm. It is here that the identity of the being is codified and its fate determined. The innate goal of any being is to prolong its life by mitigating the precursors to failure: excess risk and inefficiency. Translated into financial terms, the policy statement dictates all aspects of investment process – the mission, benchmarks and milestones; the best path with which to achieve those goals; and the decision-making process for doing so.

Each institution type has varying needs, or liabilities, that must be met perennially, and at times annually. In many cases, an investment office manages multiple capital pools with varying return targets. Depending on the legal structure, certain institution types, like endowments, can rely on inbound cash flow in the form of gifts and donations to buoy the balance sheet. Foundations, in contrast, by tax law are restricted from capital inflows and must pay out 5 percent of total asset value annually.

Like any living being, there is a unique, tailored set of guidelines for accomplishing the respective goal that is both rigid in its dictation of processes and subject to evolve and adapt in response to or in anticipation of external conditions. A chink or inefficiency in the chain can lead to unintended or adverse side effects in the overall longevity and prosperity of the life form.

Inherent in this drive to thrive is a long-term point of view, a crucial aspect in an institutional market approach.

"Long-term orientation is essential for institutional investors," said Sean Feng, investment director at Kresge Foundation. "While this principle is easy to profess, it is hard to implement. This is because of investors' herd mentality, investment managers' career risk fear and institutional constraints at many organizations."

An entity predominantly concerned with the near-term is subject to the risk of tactical error and hindsight bias. A long-term perspective, conversely, is prime to ride out cyclicality and volatility and permits taking higher liquidity risk. Overtime, that has equated to allocating a larger share of the capital base to private market strategies, an approach popularized and expertly implemented by David Swenson and the Yale University Investment Office.

"Structurally, the market's short-term focus creates 'time-horizon arbitrage' opportunities for long-term investors," Feng said. "Long-term orientation can be a sustainable competitive edge for an investment team, but only when the team has the right culture, incentive structure and long-term capital to truly implement it."

To understand the complex life form known as the sophisticated institutional investment office portfolio, it is best to break it down into its constituent parts. First is the institution's governance structure, a hierarchy of delineated processes, authority and review. Second, is the asset allocation strategy that establishes a framework for achieving the desired mission on an annual and long-term basis. Third is manager selection, or more broadly the implementation of the asset allocation strategy. The successful culmination of these three factors produces life, or, to drop the analogy, fiscal security and prosperity for the institution.

7. Governance, Due Diligence

Across the institutional investment universe, governance structures take myriad forms along the spectrums of structure and authority. Depending on the organization, this committee could be comprised of investment professionals, local officials and/or the organization's broader leadership. Many chief investment officers are endowed the authority to hire and fire managers, while others must seek board approval. The latter, combined with varying degrees of financial savvy, can sometimes create hurdles in proposing complex investment theses. This results in either an education project for the board or a simplification of the investment strategy.

In summary, much like everything else, governance is tailored to the institution, and its success is judged by its ability to foster successful stewardship of the firm's capital.

Structure

The University of Minnesota has an eight-member board of investment professionals who meet formally every quarter interspersed with regular phone meetings.

"All members are professional investors themselves in their day jobs, and they all are really committed to helping us build and manage a pretty complex portfolio," said Stuart Mason, the university's chief investment officer.

Mason echoed the importance that nearly everyone we spoke to placed on a sound, efficient and rigorous governance structure.

"An important factor to success is a governance structure that has within it a very skilled, committed and engaged investment committee," he said. "I think their engagement and their commitment really extends our ability to make good asset allocation decisions and keeps the bar high on our underwriting strategies."

A key to an ideal governance structure is a bespoke approach that emanates from governance, to investment staff to the underlying securities.

"You have to have a governance structure that gives you flexibility," he said. "You have to have the internal skills to be able to evaluate opportunities and to determine if [an investment opportunity] fits in your portfolio and adds incrementally to meeting the objectives that your endowment has established. Every one of us has a different set of objectives. What works for us may not work for one of my peers just down the street."

The investment office at Adventist Health System, a hospital system based in Altamonte Springs, Florida, manages more than $5 billion. Adventist's investment advisory committee, or IAC, has a governance model of mixed investment expertise and backgrounds, comprised of AHS senior management, members of the AHS Board Finance Committee and external investment experts.

Given their mixed level of financial expertise, the committee focuses on establishing processes and auditing performance. All investment recommendations, however, are sent to the hospital systems' board finance committee for final approval.

"The IAC focuses on larger issues pertaining to how we are trying to improve, but does not take on issues such as manager hiring or firing," said Rob Roy, the system's vice president and chief investment officer. "A larger issue for annual focus is helping to approve and set the risk levels for the funds in the context of the financial strength of AHS."

The Texas Municipal Retirement System, by contrast, has a board of trustees composed of high-ranking city officials from several Texas cities. The board approves individual investment manager selections.

"While this has faced some bottleneck challenges, given the significant number of managers we've sought approval for, the organization as a whole has risen to the challenge," said Tom Masthay, the system's director of real assets.

For Masthay and the rest of the investment team, it is a healthy exercise in explaining the investment opportunities in clear and digestible terms.

"As an investment team, we've done our best in communicating with concision, highlighting in simple two-dimensional charts or one-dimensional concepts the things our board should really be considering from a fiduciary standpoint," he said.

"For example," he said, "we may tell them in our meetings, 'Here is our portfolio before the recommendations, here is the portfolio after the recommendations and here is why we think this is the appropriate thing to do and is within the investment policy statement guidelines.'"

The largest challenge for a governance structure like the one in place at Texas Municipal and many other government-related investment offices, Masthay says, is that the board often relies on precedents.

"Fortunately, we came into an organization that was forward-thinking and were able to build a lot of trust by getting our work done, improving performance and really doing our best to meet all the objectives of the organization," he said. "TMRS has – by light-years – the most effective public board I've worked for."

Authority & Due Diligence

Of the 45 institutional investors that discussed governance in their interviews with Trusted Insight, 21 chief investment officers held investment authority, the power to hire and fire managers. While we do not suggest this random sampling is representative of the broader industry, the roughly even split of authority offered diverse examples of governance structures. The dichotomy of who holds decision-making authority is not as cut and dry as right or wrong, and throughout our conversations clear themes emerged highlighting the advantages and drawbacks of each model.

A commonality is the description of an in-depth vetting procedure initiated months prior and culminating in the presentation of a qualitative, quantitative and legal argument for the manager's viability and expected value to the portfolio.

The Maine Public Employees' Retirement System board has final say on all investments. Leading up to that point is an intensive diligence process. For any given investment, one investment team member takes lead on a formalized procedure of interviews, information gathering and legal analysis. Then the investment is submitted to the broader team for peer review, and finally, it is presented to the board.

"At the time of the trustee vote, we've nailed down about 85 percent of the work on an investment, and the other 15 percent is just final due diligence items and final legal negotiations," said Barley Parker, managing director of real estate at the pension fund. "Each approval from the trustees is always subject to us getting through those final items."

The Yale-New Haven Health System investment office must also seek board approval. However, before the board is asked to judge, all members of the investment staff must buy in.

That kicks off an routine that Bill Camelio, a Yale-New Haven investment strategist, describes as "an iterative process between the investment staff, investment committee and our consultant."

"We will attend industry specific forums and education sessions to help ensure we know the current market environment," Camelio said. "We will meet with a number of firms to understand their process and philosophy, including multiple meetings with portfolio managers and analysts."

Sometimes seeking board approval means teaching the committee the purpose and value of an investment. Take the Employees' Retirement System of Texas and its former hedge funds director Robert C. Lee for instance.

"Over the last five years, we've gone through a lot of education with the board and staff to show them the "synergies" of having these types of investments," Lee said in an July 2016 interview before ultimately leaving the retirement system in September 2016. "We've been successful in doing that."

Over that period, Lee and the team met their 5 percent absolute return target allocation and began utilizing hedge funds for other asset classes. That success is thanks, at least in part, to the investment team's ability of enumerating the strategic value of hedge funds.

"…It was a controlled experiment for the board and staff to figure out "what is a hedge fund? How can it be useful to the plan and what are the ancillary benefits of having hedge funds as part of our investment group?" Lee said.

At the UJA-Federation of New York, a $1.28 billion endowment, Chief Investment Officer Collin Ambrose holds decision-making authority.

"We have a long-term orientation and buy-in from our committee on our strategic policy portfolio and the risk-return objectives for the pool of capital," Ambrose said. "We have targets and ranges for how we want to allocate capital, and we don't concern ourselves with short-term volatility."

Nonetheless, Ambrose keeps his board informed and engaged to ensure buy-in on potential investments.

"Typically, we review what we think could go wrong ahead of time and discuss our potential concerns upfront," he said. "Conversely, we discuss circumstances where we would add to a strategy. So, when we see a pullback and the opportunity is still attractive, we are able to put additional money to work."

Sam Masoudi, chief investment officer of the Wyoming Retirement System, is similarly endowed with manager hiring authority. To keep the board informed, Masoudi and his team craft extensive due diligence memos for every new investment after the investment is made.

"The main benefit is that we don't have to wait for quarterly meetings to get investments approved, and we don't have to spend quite as much time debating the merits of the investments with the board as we might have to otherwise," he said. "I think it also makes it less of a political process. We can make investments based purely on the merits."

The Northwest Area Foundation has an investment team of one. It also manages to have a robust private markets portfolio, which requires considerable due diligence.

To ensure a timely process, the investment committee delegates investment authority to Amy Jensen, the lone investment director. Instead, the committee sets the high-level priorities and direction of the portfolio.

"This allows me to do things that may surprise people," Jensen said. "I can really prioritize something and complete investments on tight timelines."

She, however, is not merely selecting private market managers, but also spearheading co-investment opportunities. "Some people would say, 'With a staff of one, you would never have the ability to do that,'" she said. "We have a great governance structure that allows me to work really quickly in a way that some very large organizations with much larger staffs couldn't do because they need committee approval. That is an advantage."

Underlying the various interpretations of an ideal governance structure is the need for *a system*, any system as long as it is clearly defined and logically suits the institution's needs, that mitigates its weaknesses and empowers the investment staff to uphold their fiduciary responsibilities.

"A good governance structure starts with a clear articulation of roles and responsibilities," UJA Federation's Colin Ambrose said. "It is critically important that the investment committee and the investment office work closely together and have the same risk-return objectives and tolerance for drawdowns in the portfolio."

"A bad governance structure can also be part and parcel a bad investment process," said Lawrence Kochard, chief investment officer and CEO at the University of Virginia Investment Management Company, or UVIMCO. "If you find an institution that tends to, when the markets are going well, be adding risk, and it might be that they're adding risk because they felt like their performance had been lagging peers. When the market's doing really badly, all of a sudden they de-risk. That's kind of a symptom of a bad governance structure."

At UVIMCO, which was spun out as a separate management company in 2004, the investment committee sets the investment policy statement and overall philosophy. Kochard, however, holds investment authority within the constraints of the policy statement.

"What makes that work is making sure that there's a high level of quality information that we provide to the board to make them comfortable that we're living up to what we had promised," he said.

To revive the original metaphor, the investment policy, fine-tuned to support long-term (fiscal) health, is the crucial element without which any governing committee is doomed to fall ill.

"A good governance is one that enables you to think long-term and manage risk appropriately, meaning keep it within a pretty tight band, never getting too euphoric or never getting too negative, but making sure it stays consistent with the risk tolerance of the institution and truly thinking long term," Kochard said. "All these are commonsense things that people say they do, or try to do. When that doesn't occur, it's usually the result of a bad governance process."

The process for diagnosing health of the investment office is simple:

"As opposed to just saying that, 'XYZ institution is bad, and this one's good,' I think it's really more looking at the symptoms," Kochard said. "If you look at the symptoms and you see what I laid out, that's more indicative of a bad governance for an institution.

Thus the optimal outcome in any situation is to rely on the governance structure. "An issue of key importance in all markets, but especially in down markets, is to have the right governance and a good board or investment committee that can stay the course, that understands that down markets will happen and that stay with the strategic plan," said Kim Walker, former chief investment officer at Washington University Investment Management Company, who resigned in December 2016.

8. Asset Allocation

Fairly ubiquitous across endowments, foundations, pension funds, health systems and even some family offices managing $1 billion or more is a variation of what became known as "the endowment model." This is a portfolio with around six equally weighted asset classes with a preference for maximizing illiquid, often private market, assets.

To understand how these strategies have developed in the past decade, it's important to recognize the lasting impact that the great recession and the resulting actions that followed had on institutional investors.

To resuscitate the economy, the Federal Reserve implemented multiple rounds of quantitative easing, which increased the supply of money and artificially lowered interest rates. These actions were eventually repeated by governments around the world. This fueled a historic stock market bull run from its bottom in 2009 that tapered to largely trading sideways by January 2015 and through the following two years. Outlooks for continued low-growth resulted in a search for alpha in assets like private equity and venture capital. Over the same period, historically low interest rates coupled with new regulations requiring banks to maintain a certain amount of liquidity rendered public debt less desirable and opened a market in the private credit space where banks used to dominate.

"Because they've stratified the economy, the rate of return on normal publicly traded investments is going to be low," said Mark Canavan, senior portfolio manager at the New Mexico Educational Retirement Board. "Stock markets are not going to provide the performance they did during the 80s or 90s. It's not going to have the historical 8 or 9 percent rate of return. Bonds aren't going to deliver for sure, and even the private equity markets have gotten pretty compressed."

Those fiscal and regulatory actions to rebound quickly from economic collapse created long tailwinds that equate to a market environment unlike anything anyone has ever seen before.

"It really scares me," Canavan said. "...I'm concerned that this is a policy market. It is not driven by economics. This market is driven by policy, specifically interest rate policy, monetary policy. That's what's keeping the market up."

At his previous employer, the New Mexico State Treasury, Canavan was able to stumble his way to the conclusion that the global economy was on the brink of collapse in 2007. He derisked the institution's portfolio and largely avoided the worst of the meltdown.

"My call at the Treasurer's Office was based on boatloads of anecdotal experience, and my looking at a situation going, 'Wow, this looks just like back then, except worse,'" he said. "Right now, I don't have any anecdotal roadmap to tell me what goes from here, and it scares me."

Carol McFate pointed to persistently low interest rates and central bank involvement in markets for an increased focus on liabilities and hedging. The 2016 presidential election, she said, has since shifted the valuation model for certain assets. "Before the U.S. election, interest rates kept dropping and risk assets soared to new levels, and conventional valuation metrics led to the view that markets were generally overvalued. Then, post-election, interest rates started to rise in anticipation of higher growth and inflation, while equities continued to rise. The conventional way of looking at valuation keeps changing, so being sensitive to your largest risk contributor, interest rates, is even more important."

"It's challenging because you can't look at any asset class through the lens of historical expectations," McFate said. "You have to be aware of the context in which you're living, and what that could mean for asset returns."

For David Barcus, this unprecedented environment has led him to adapt quickly.

"Having come into this industry right before the financial crisis, there really is not such a thing as a normal investing environment, so the ability to constantly evaluate where you are has proven to be critical."

Boil these variables down and you have an increasingly competitive private market environment and an industry-wide search for niche, differentiated strategies.

Due to its increased prominence and general opaqueness, our conversations disproportionately favored discussion about private markets. Nonetheless, there was a general reversion to the thesis that strategic asset allocation, not security selection, drives returns over the long-term.

An asset allocation strategy stems from the institution's mission, the size of its capital base and its desired rate of return versus its maximum risk and illiquidity tolerances. Those factors are then parsed through the CIO and investment committee's investment philosophies to form a unique portfolio design outlined in the investment policy statement.

If the investment policy is an institution's DNA, then the asset allocation strategy is the firm's nutritional plan, the managers are chefs and the underlying securities are the food. Like a nutritional plan does for the edible world, an asset allocation policy divides the investable universe into particular groups and details what percentage of those groups garner the highest probability of long-term stability and vitality. And there are numerous ways of viewing a portfolio -- by traditional asset classes, by liquidity, by risk or by assigning broad buckets, like public versus private. I will discontinue the analogy here to avoid the temptation of calling something the Atkin's Diet of allocation strategies.

Tailored & Long-Term

Pension funds have an annual liability to negate or outpace. To qualify for tax benefits, foundations are required to distribute a minimum of 5 percent of asset value each year. Investment offices at hospital systems, insurance companies and corporations must grapple with the implications of being one aspect of a complex balance sheet. University endowments cover varying percentages of operational and project costs. Family offices and sovereign wealth funds can enjoy the most liquidity freedom with virtually no near-term liability and a concentrated constituency.

"The biggest thing in my mind is the investment approach really needs to be tailored to the circumstances of the institution you serve," said Bob Jacksha, chief investment officer at the New Mexico Educational Retirement Board. "Certainly that was drummed into us on the buy side, where suitability is always an issue. It's something that I've seen more and more over my career."

For Jacksha and the broader public pension fund segment, that means a narrow path defined by restrictions and the annual liability, which is where strong governance and asset allocation become vital.

"Being on the institutional side means that you have to follow rules, regulations, legal constraints, policies, that sort of thing," Jacksha said. "On the other hand, I think you need to have policies and practices that allow you enough flexibility to take advantage of opportunities when they're there and to avoid pitfalls when they become apparent."

In Robert Maynard's four-decade investment career, he has seen many investment trends and fads come and go, at times shaping the industry. As chief investment officer at Public Employees' Retirement System Of Idaho, Maynard has devised a system that works for the pension.

"For the most part, I have come to conclusion there's a thousand ways to invest," Maynard said. "The key is trying to find the best way to invest given your institution or constituency's history and traditions. I put a high premium on explainability."

Maynard points to Chief Investment Officer Matt Clark's in-house tactical approach at the South Dakota Investment Council, which he "...is probably the best in the world at..." or the Washington State investment office's private equity prowess, dating back to the 90s. For Maynard, it's all about simplicity and sticking to the plan.

"Depending upon your constituency and the history of your institution, the key is keeping with an approach over a prolonged period of time," he said. "That means five-to-ten years at the very least. You've got to choose the investment approach that's most appropriate and explainable to your constituency."

"Our mantra is simple, transparent, focused and patient," Maynard reiterated. "We are a two-person operation with a small back office. Being able to explain what we do in times of crisis and keeping the constituency on course has achieved great value for us."

Beyond a certain point, adding complexity to the portfolio doesn't increase returns, Maynard said, which is all the more reason to keep it simple.

"New things come up from time to time, as is the case with the market at the moment," he said. "It's not a matter of fact, it's a matter of faith as to whether they add returns after the additional fees. It is difficult to beat the market, but that also means that it is difficult for a professionally diversified portfolio to lose too much, so long as you're not doing anything really stupid, like betting it all on red."

That is the luxury that institutions can afford that other market participants aren't privy to: a long-term investment horizon.

"One of the benefits of being at a foundation is the long-term view that we are enabled to take," said Dean Duchak, director of investments at the Kaiser Family Foundation. "We have one pool of capital that is a permanent pool of capital, theoretically indefinite, and really investing through that view allows us to take a long-term perspective when we're looking at ideas."

9. Investment Philosophy

Trusted Insight estimates that there are 4,400 institutional investment offices globally controlling roughly $40 to $45 trillion. Of that, we estimate that $8 trillion of that is allocated to alternatives. To put it in general terms, there is a near-infinite supply of capital chasing a finite number of investments. The natural progression of thought suggests institutions will form a herd that drive the markets, a premise which anecdotally seems to hold merit.

Nonetheless, there is variance between the portfolios of institution A and institution B, even if they are nearly identical on every other front. This can be attributed to a concept that we'll refer to as investment philosophy. Stated plainly, investment philosophy is the human element of investment management wrapped around the institution's needs. Every investment office is comprised of unique individuals with varying backgrounds, views and expertise. It's those variables that play a critical, yet hard to define, role in portfolio construction.

Philip Rotner was part of the Massachusetts Institute of Technology Investment Management Company for more than 17 years before being hired as the inaugural chief investment officer by Boston Children's Hospital in May 2010 to build a sophisticated investment office.

"My goal was—and is—to build a first-class team by recruiting quality people as well as to hire some younger staff and build talent," Rotner said. "Simultaneously, we built out a more proprietary portfolio that meets the needs of the hospital from a risk and return perspective. The portfolio is built around what we consider some of the best attributes of high quality endowment portfolio management."

Despite referring to his portfolio in reference to the endowment model structure, the Boston Children's portfolio is a unique entity shaped by Rotner's views and past experiences and those of his team.

"Like most things in life, it is the people that distinguish us," said Philip Rotner, chief investment officer at Boston Children's Hospital. "People can articulate the same strategy, but execute it differently."

For Jonathan Grabel, the former chief investment officer of the Public Employee's Retirement Association of New Mexico, investment philosophy is frame of mind filtered through the spectrum of the particular institution.

"A lot of other organizations, whether they are a pension, endowment or foundation, think of themselves as investors first," Grabel said. "We think ourselves as public servants first, with a very important mission, and we invest in that context."

"Our mission is to preserve, protect and administer the trust to meet its current and future obligations," he explained. "That is pretty simple phrasing, but it means that you have to be both passionate and dispassionate, and balance current and future needs."

A defining variable of Grabel's view toward investment management at New Mexico was the pension fund's liability, which is growing steadily.

"Consequently, we take maintenance of liquidity very seriously," he said. "As a mature pension, we are cash flow negative; member and employer contributions are in the magnitude of $500 million a year, and our benefit payouts are $1 billion a year. We pay out over $80 million-plus a month, and so we need to make sure that we have sufficient liquidity for that. We do not want to be in a position where we are a forced seller of securities in order to pay benefits."

That burden, plus a critically analytical disposition, fuels the New Mexico team and shapes their every decision.

"I think what keeps us focused on our mission is that we have a certain amount of humility and rigorous processes in terms of challenging every assumption, be it at the asset allocation level or within asset categories. This is opposed to arrogantly thinking we can beat any benchmark, or that tactically we know what's going to happen in the markets on any given day," Grabel said in a January 2016 interview, before leaving the pension in April 2017.

Investment philosophies and asset allocations are inherently theoretical. There is no right answer and everything is premised on underlying assumptions.

"...The average institutional investor is too willing to conventionally fail," said Tom Masthay, director of real assets at the Texas Municipal Retirement System, who attributed this logic to his colleague. "And because of that, to a large extent public pension plans have very similar asset allocations and operate in bureaucratic molds that none of the investment managers, endowments, family offices, sovereign wealth funds or other industry players seek to emulate."

Masthay attributes this herd mentality to long-accepted assumptions that predicate many investment theses.

"I think that whole concept of Markowitz strategic asset allocation needs to be challenged," Masthay said. "Obviously we have an institutional framework within which we operate, but we're thinking through these things on a daily basis."

In practical terms for Masthay, that means "we try to make fewer decisions, not more, and to simplify our thinking, not complicate. We have been in a period of rapid diversification compared with a just-bonds-only portfolio in 2009. So, admittedly there is a bit of a juxtaposition in our approach. Institutional investors can probably do things simpler. Although, I would say alternative asset classes play an important part in asset allocation going forward."

In the end, no matter the investor's previous experiences, everything boils down serving the institution. Lorrie Tingle, chief investment officer at the Public Employees' Retirement System of Mississippi, puts it best:

"I would argue selecting the right investment approach isn't a one-size-fits-all decision. In deciding on the appropriate investment model for a plan, I believe every CIO has to look at their particular situation, including plan funding, participant demographics, annual liquidity needs and their available staff resources to identify the approach that makes sense for their plan long term."

10. Dimensions Of Dissecting A Portfolio

For some institutions, liquidity is the primary driver of asset allocation. For sovereign wealth funds and family offices, liquidity is less important (on a relative basis) than measured, aggressive approaches to generate returns. This isn't to suggest that any given institution doesn't seek diversification to achieve long-term growth and security. These are, however, outliers on either end of the liquidity spectrum, with most firm types falling somewhere in between.

Thus, there are various means to dissect a portfolio, defined by the prioritization of an institution's desire for maximizing returns, minimizing risk and determining the appropriate level of liquidity with which to achieve those goals.

The first is to divide the investable universe by asset class. The second is to group investments into broad buc t of acceptable portfolio risk. The final strategy is one viewed from the perspective of liquidity. It is important to note that these groupings are based on the predominant variable through which a portfolio is viewed. Fundamental to all institutions is to achieve some degree of diversification through efficient asset allocation across public and private markets, and a consideration of risk, return and liquidity is inherently universal.

Asset Class

At its most basic level, assets can be codified in three simple categories: equity, debt and cash. Assets can be further broken down into traditional -- public equities, fixed income and cash -- and alternatives -- real assets, private equity and absolute return. Asset classes differ in terms of legal liabilities, liquidity and risk-return profiles. Depending on the institution's risk tolerance level and return pressure, most investors divide capital among multiple asset classes to ensure reliable, cost-effective returns while earning market-beating profits when opportunities prevail.

Carnegie Mellon University embarked on an ambitious plan to diversify into new markets a little over a decade ago. Now, the endowment, which is structured along asset class lines, has a strong presence in private markets.

"We are over-allocated on some asset classes and under-allocated on others," said

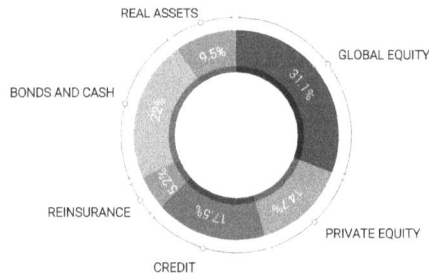

UNIVERSITY OF MINNESOTA FOUNDATION ASSET ALLOCATION

REAL ASSETS
GLOBAL EQUITY
BONDS AND CASH
9.5%
31.1%
22%
5.2%
REINSURANCE
17.5%
14.7%
PRIVATE EQUITY
CREDIT

Source: University of Minnesota Endowment Website (as of Dec. 31, 2016)

Charles Kennedy, the endowment's chief investment officer. "Overall, we are looking to be a pretty steady state with respect to having a significant allocation of around 30 percent to private equity, defined as venture capital, growth and buyouts."

The University of Minnesota Foundation spends 4.5 percent of asset value annually to fund university operation costs. To achieve reliable, predictable returns, its portfolio is broken into six segments that span public and private markets.

The global equity allocation is the largest segment at 31 percent, which consists primarily of indexed funds. This allows the university's investment staff to focus on private market deals.

"At the University, our strategy has been to have nearly 50 percent in private fund structures, do it all direct and really underwrite very aggressively a variety of private investments where the expectation is high for added value," said Chief Investment Officer Stuart Mason.

The UJA-Federation endowment allocates nearly half of investable capital to public markets and close to the other half in private markets.

"We have an equity-biased portfolio that's diversified by asset class, strategy and manager," said Colin Ambrose, chief investment officer. "We designed our portfolio to achieve attractive returns throughout market cycles, while minimizing the risk of permanent impairment of capital. As investors with a permanent capital base, we focus on the long term and are able to tolerate short-term mark-to-market volatility. Our long-term mindset matches our capital, which is intended to last for generations. As patient investors, we don't worry about short-term market gyrations or focus on short-term performance.

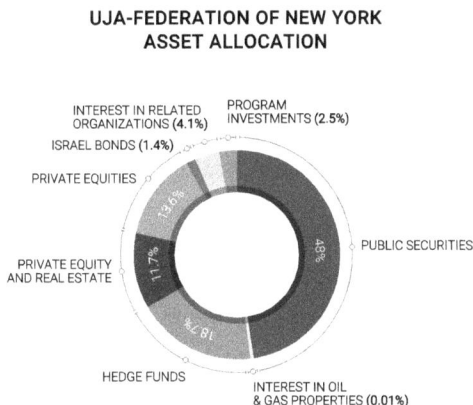

UJA-FEDERATION OF NEW YORK ASSET ALLOCATION

INTEREST IN RELATED ORGANIZATIONS (4.1%)
PROGRAM INVESTMENTS (2.5%)
ISRAEL BONDS (1.4%)
PRIVATE EQUITIES
PRIVATE EQUITY AND REAL ESTATE — 11.7%
13.6%
PUBLIC SECURITIES — 49%
18.7%
HEDGE FUNDS
INTEREST IN OIL & GAS PROPERTIES (0.01%)

Source: Tax Filings (year ending Jun. 30, 2015)

On the private side of things, those assets break down into roughly 19 percent in hedge funds, 12 percent in private real estate and 14 percent in private equity.

"In a low-return environment, beta is not providing enough returns, and investors are focused on extracting alpha from their hedge funds and allocating more to private equity," Ambrose said. "It's not a change for us as we have half of our portfolio invested in alpha-seeking hedge funds and private equity strategies. We continue to invest in private capital strategies so we can take advantage of the liquidity premium as long-term investors."

Steve Edmundson is the sole investment professional at the Public Employees' Retirement System of Nevada, a $35 billion pension fund with a fairly simplistic portfolio strategy.

The portfolio is broken into five segments: domestic equity, domestic fixed income, international equity, cash and private markets investments. In stark contrast to the endowment model, the pension only allocates 8.7 percent to private markets. The rest are in public markets.

"It's a fairly conservative structure," Edmundson said. "Our private real estate allocation entirely consists of unlevered, fully-leased core assets, which is also consistent with our total fund structure. We have a focus on high-quality assets throughout the fund, including our private markets allocation. The Nevada model has really become synonymous with simplicity with a focus on keeping costs low and an emphasis on high-quality assets. That kind of high-quality bias is consistent throughout the fund, not just in our private market's allocation."

Edmundson notes that absent from the portfolio are any hedge funds, "an overt decision" by himself and the investment committee.

"...We see hedge funds more as a management style rather than a specific asset class and have never been comfortable with the complexity, lack of transpar-

PUBLIC EMPLOYEES' RETIREMENT SYSTEM OF NEVADA ASSET ALLOCATION

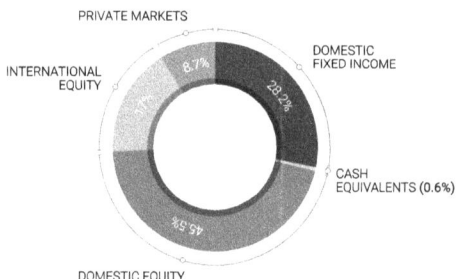

PRIVATE MARKETS

DOMESTIC FIXED INCOME

INTERNATIONAL EQUITY

8.7%

28.2%

CASH EQUIVALENTS (0.6%)

45.5%

DOMESTIC EQUITY

Source: Financial Statement (as of Mar. 31, 2017)

ency and fee structure associated with hedge funds," he said. "They just haven't found a spot. Hedge funds aren't consistent with our overall high-quality, simple approach to investing."

Buckets

Sometimes asset classes are too narrow a description by which to divide a portfolio. Instead, some institutions categorize assets by their defining characteristics or desired outcomes.

The simplest denomination of buckets it public versus private. When Bob Jacksha was hired in 2007, the New Mexico Educational Retirement Board was nearly 70 percent in public equities. Since then, he has led a diversification of the portfolio among public equity, fixed income and alternative assets.

NEW MEXICO EDUCATIONAL RETIREMENT BOARD ASSET ALLOCATION

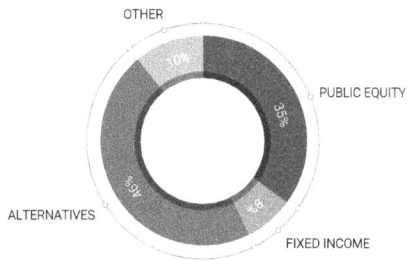

Source: NMERB Asset Liability Study (as of Jun. 24, 2016)

"We added a lot of alternative asset classes, and we now have probably one of the more diverse portfolios you'll see in public pension plans," Jacksha said. "We found these strategies worked and served us well in the recent volatility."

At the end of fiscal year 2016, the pension fund targeted an allocation of 35 percent public equity, 8 percent fixed income, 46 percent alternatives and 10 percent to a loosely defined bucket that includes risk parity and global assets. This strategy allocates nearly twice as much capital to alternative markets as the average asset allocation for pension funds managing more than $1 billion, according to the fund's 2016 asset liability study.

With funding levels below an acceptable level, Jacksha said the broad market diversity is crucial to keeping the pension on sound financial footing.

"We realize that we do certainly give up a little bit of upside in the real strong bull markets in U.S. stocks, but being an underfunded pension plan, you just can't afford a big drawdown," Jacksha said. "That could be catastrophic, and we've tried to avoid that. Knock on wood--so far so good. We've dampened the volatility in the portfolio."

The W.K. Kellogg Foundation's Chief Investment Officer Joel Wittenberg said the diversified portfolio invests across all asset classes, but they classify them by "various risk exposures, liquidity, deflation and inflation, with the largest portion in capital appreciation assets." An underlying investment theme for Kellogg "is a cash flow and value bias."

AVERAGE PUBLIC PENSIONS WITH AUM OVER $1B ASSET ALLOCATION

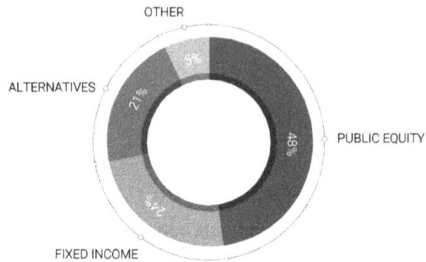

OTHER 5%
ALTERNATIVES 21%
PUBLIC EQUITY 48%
FIXED INCOME 24%

Source: NMERB Asset Liability Study (as of Jun. 24, 2016)

What that translates to: 61.2 percent of the $9.2 billion foundation is invested in Kellogg stock; a roughly even distribution of single-digit allocations to commingled funds, public equity, hedge funds and private equity; and small allotments for fixed income, real estate and cash.

The Northwest Area Foundation portfolio consists of four large beta buckets: equity; fixed income and credit; real assets; and then diversifying strategies, which are strategies that have low beta to those other parts of the portfolio.

"We have a broader asset allocation than most organizations," said Amy Jensen, the foundation's sole investor. "... That flexibility has allowed us to be a lot more opportunistic

W.K. KELLOGG FOUNDATION ASSET ALLOCATION

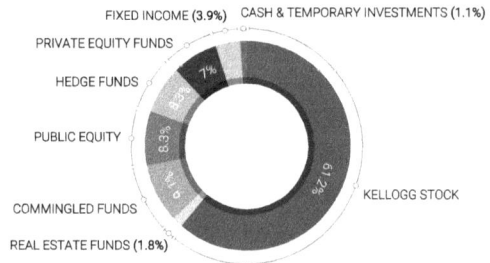

FIXED INCOME (3.9%)   CASH & TEMPORARY INVESTMENTS (1.1%)
PRIVATE EQUITY FUNDS
HEDGE FUNDS 7%
PUBLIC EQUITY 8.3%
COMMINGLED FUNDS
REAL ESTATE FUNDS (1.8%)
KELLOGG STOCK 61.2%

Source: 2016 Annual Report (as of Aug. 31, 2016)

than most organizations. By the nature of how they're designed, they have much tighter controls on their allocation. It's given the committee flexibility to be more opportunistic and more strategic. It's given me an opportunity to think about the portfolio differently and add differentiated strategies."

Risk

The Howard Hughes Medical Institute endowment supports 100 percent of the institution's spending. With that in mind, risk is at the forefront of the allocation strategy.

"I think that gives us a different view about risk," said Mark Barnard, who served as managing director of private investments for more than 25 years before retiring in June 2016. "Volatility is not our friend because our business is to employ top-notch scientists in biomedical research with long-term research projects that are not easy to turn on and off. So, we have a slightly different risk profile than some of the other endowments."

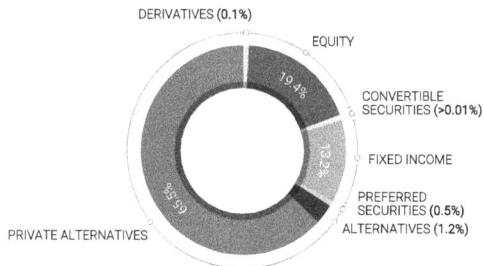

HOWARD HUGHES MEDICAL INSTITUTE ASSET ALLOCATION

Source: HHMI Financial Statement (as of Aug. 31, 2016)

The institute allocates more than 65 percent of assets to alternative investments, which constitutes private equity; hedge funds; distressed and credit sensitive investments; equity commingled funds; real assets; and market neutral investments. Fixed income and public equities account for 13 percent and 19 percent, respectively.

"I would say that the portfolio is positioned more defensively now than it has been in a while," Barnard said. "There are few easy opportunities anywhere right now. There may be some coming in the debt markets due to the stress in mining and energy. We still have the majority of our assets in alternative investments. We have some strategies that we think can create equity-like returns with less volatility, and some where we expect higher alpha, but are overall still defensive."

Some institutions have taken the concept of risk management to a new level.

When Chris Halaska was named chief investment officer and senior vice president of the Memorial Hermann Healthcare System in October 2012, he inherited a portfolio that was nearly 85 percent cash and fixed income. Since then, the investment team has "almost the exact inverse of that, with 23 percent cash and fixed income."

"Because of the legacy allocation, we had a clean slate, drew up a new IPS, new investment committee charter and re-engineered a more modern endowment-style asset allocation," Halaska said.

With this blank check, Halaska and his team decided that risk management would be the defining factor of the portfolio, which currently consists of approximately 40 percent in capital preservation-style investments, 40 percent in growth and 20 percent in real return strategies.

"We use risk factoring framework in terms of how we think about asset classes versus the more traditional cash, fixed income, equities, alternatives," he said. "So for example, hedge funds are not in the alternatives bucket. They go in either the "growth" allocation or "capital preservation" allocation, depending on how they perform under different economic environments."

For Lawrence Kochard and UVIMCO, there are no target allocations. Instead, the endowment has a risk budget that can be allotted across asset classes.

"We have an overall level of market risk that we manage to that's consistent with our policy portfolio," Kochard said. "All public -- equities, bonds and real estate -- can be done passively, and we manage a level of drawdown risk that's consistent with that. Then we have a level of liquidity risk that we think of in terms of what is the most liquid we can become and still feel comfortable? As opposed to targeting private equity, we just target the level of risk assets that we want, as well as level of liquidity."

This strategy, Kochard argues, allows you to compare the merits of any number of seemingly unrelated assets through the common variable of risk.

"It forces you to make these comparisons of how does this real estate fund stack up compared to a venture capital fund?" he said. "Even though it looks like apples and oranges, it forces you to make those types of comparisons in a really interesting, intellectual exercise. That may be a little different than what others are doing.

Jonathan Grabel also takes a risk-oriented, orthogonal approach to portfolio construction. He argues that there are only three main asset classes, which can be further collated by their defining characteristics.

"I do not subscribe to the traditional versus alternatives view of investments," Grabel said. "I think that there are three main asset categories: equities, fixed income and real assets. You can further divide those categories into liquid and illiquid structures, and there may be further wrinkles depending on whether a mandate is long-only or long-short."

Similar to UVIMCO, Grabel does not have a target allocation for each asset class, which he says leads to better performance in the long run.

"Consequently, we focus on the predominant risk factor associated with the major asset categories, as opposed to the wrapper or vehicle in which an investment product resides," he said. "Fundamentally, the equity risk premium or equity beta is the main driver of equity returns. The underlying portfolio construct, be it low volatility, hedge or illiquid, is a second order determinant of returns."

From that perspective, the New Mexico investment team can take a holistic view of the portfolio, review the risk and exposure metrics of each investment and make tweaks at the manager level.

"Rather than looking at the PERA fund as a pool of separate and distinct managers, we now view as more like a single consolidated pool," Grabel said. "We have tightened guidelines for all of our managers. Our risk programs help us to make sure our managers stay within their mandate and do not stray. Toward this end, we focus on more granular data and have security-level view of the portfolio as well as a top-down view. As a former technology investor, I am a big believer in the ability to harness and analyze information. We have much better data than ever before and have a better hold on all our positions across the portfolio, managers and strategies."

Following a 2014 asset allocation review, Grabel was able to reduce to portfolio's beta to under one, from a beta value greater than one previously. This was accomplished by reducing domestic equity exposure by 10 percent, separating credit from rates and investing further into private assets.

"The best diversification and risk management is potentially at the asset category level," Grabel said. "Rather than having a core fixed income portfolio that had 30 percent in high yield or emerging market debt, that's now a separate portfolio that we manage and benchmark appropriately."

Liquidity

For some institutions, liquidity takes priority over other aspects of the portfolio. These institutions either face recurring short-term payout requirements, such as charitable foundation, or, quite the opposite, they operate on a truly long-term horizon, such as single-family offices and sovereign wealth funds.

A major advantage of single-family offices and sovereign wealth funds is the enormous capital base and almost no near-term liabilities. For example, Andrew Eberhart works for a prestigious single-family office that is able to take a truly long-term perspective, and as a private capital source, it has none of the red tape that other firms must adhere to.

Eberhart relies on indexes and a small cohort of outside managers to provide broad beta across all asset classes. "This allows us to focus our internal efforts on the wealth creation (alpha) side of the portfolio, which in recent years has been focused on niche strategies, seeding of new managers and direct investments," Eberhart said.

"Niche strategies are implemented through small funds or managers with a particular expertise in an inefficient market. Examples of this might include asset leasing, structured settlements, appraisal rights or uniquely structured lending.

"We believe that to truly add value, you need to continuously deploy capital in inefficient and undeveloped markets.

"With respect to seeding new managers, we have invested with several start-up funds that we believe have the skill set to both manage money and grow their companies. In return for serving as an anchor investor, we receive a percentage of the firm's total revenue, but typically we do not seek ownership. This structure has a double bottom line in that we receive an investment return on the funds we have invested, while also benefitting from the firm's overall growth via revenue sharing.

"Finally, with direct deals, we generally co-invest with other private investors and/or venture and private equity funds. We avoid early-stage deals and technology risk and are particularly interested in special situations where we have a competitive advantage. While these deals are research intensive and highly illiquid, they are also the opportunities that can deliver outsized returns."

Yup Kim, senior portfolio manager at the Alaska Permanent Fund, a $55 billion sovereign wealth fund, said it's a major advantage across the board to have no near-term liability. "There's a deeper appreciation about our ability to leverage the stability and scale of our capital base," he said. "Given the absence of a ticking clock to satisfy an annual liability stream, we're able to pursue opportunities which require the resilience to stomach short-term volatility, those which require a longer-term, ten plus year investment horizon or those that don't fit neatly into an asset class category. As it relates to our scale, we're able to be more assertive and negotiate beneficial terms and better risk-adjusted return matrices through enhanced term sheets or investment structures."

On the flip side, foundations must pay out regular liabilities, which often equates to a more liquid portfolio.

Washington University Investment Management Company, located in St. Louis, Missouri, is organized around liquidity. Mark Newcomb, for instance, is the team's director of liquid public market strategies, which includes liquid credits, equities, rates and currencies. The remainder of the portfolio is split into illiquid private market investments and absolute return.

"In the endowment, we're quite unconstrained with how we invest," Newcomb said. "We just have a very high constraining hurdle, which focuses our attention in certain areas."

"Working in buckets," Newcomb argues, "is not going to achieve our goal in the prospective future." And he says viewing a portfolio with liquidity at top of mind is a fundamental shift in investment management.

"Endowments are getting a lot more creative in the kinds of investments that are out there in order to deliver on their promised goals to their university."

"...The investment world has evolved so much that just finding simple ideas that you can bucket into those is challenging. Investments just don't fall into that, so you're looking at other kinds of ways to understand, categorize and manage. Those might be in the form of liquidity or illiquidity, different geographies or what you have.

I think endowments, in general, are moving toward that more unconstrained, creative way that they can better deploy capital. It's like a process improvement mentality that endowments are starting to get really acute with, because it's going to be a lot more difficult environment for the next 10 years than the last 10."

11. Manager Selection

The investment policy statement is set with a clearly defined investment philosophy and asset allocation strategy. What's left is implementation--into either actively or passively managed strategies. With an increased institutional presence in private markets and a dearth of hard metrics underlying many of these investments, our conversations focused on the key determinants of successfully selecting private market asset managers.

The most basic factor is the size of the institution's capital base and thus the minimum and maximum check sizes that can be written. From there, it's crucial to have a stable team, a repeatable process and a verifiable track record. Beyond that is an ever increasing search for niche strategies. To find those, the capital allocators we spoke with overwhelmingly said they seek strong partnerships with trustworthy managers that have an edge, with a preference toward managers earlier in their life cycle.

AUM & Check Size

Many funds managing less than $1 billion can't afford a sophisticated in-house investment office and must rely on outsourced investors and/or indexing. For funds in the tens (and hundreds) of billions of dollars, there is a minimum amount of money that must be committed to each deal in order to make the investment economically worthwhile, which limits the number of managers that can be pursued. The goldilocks zone lay near the single-digit billion-dollar AUM range.

At more than $6 billion, Emory University endowment is one such goldilocks portfolio. "...We are at a nice place to be able to invest in smaller boutique funds," said Chief Investment Officer Mary Cahill. "Also, we are large enough that we have an investment team to find those managers. In many universities, it's not until you get to $1 billion dollars, maybe $2 billion, before you start to see investment professionals in house and of enough size to be able to find those types of investments. Also, on the illiquid side, buyouts, venture capital and hedge funds take a lot of work. You need people who are able to do that and size. We're not too large or too small."

Since markets, particularly private ones, are access constrained, it pays to have a capital base of a certain size. Stuart Mason cites the University of Minnesota's $2.2 billion in investable assets as a major benefit in today's investment climate.

"Given our size, we can make commitments to smaller funds in almost any asset class," Mason said. "Often our $10 million commitment, for example, to a private fund is meaningful to the fund manager, and if they actually do well, it can be meaningful to us. It 'moves the needle.'"

Those investments, Mason says, have a higher likelihood of producing strong returns over the long term.

"There's a lot of research that suggests smaller funds do better than larger funds in virtually every asset class," he said. "That's one reason we seek out funds that are $100 million or $250 million, and we generally avoid funds that are $2 billion or $10 billion. We don't do those because it's virtually impossible in our mind to get a three-times-your-money back on a $10 billion fund, like some of the mega private equity funds.

If you're a venture fund raising $100 million and you execute the strategy with success, then it only takes one investment to return the fund or return a multiple of the fund. While our strategy differs somewhat for each of the asset classes, across the board, you could say that we seek niche opportunities that are often addressed by smaller fund managers.

Our expectation is when we do the underwriting of each of these, that we are underwriting with an expectation of some return that is, almost always, significantly higher than just the mean for that asset class."

David Barcus, investment manager at Denison University's $750 million endowment, says the firm's sub $1 billion asset size isn't a hindrance.

"I believe we are at a sweet spot where we are big enough to be viewed as a meaningful LP to GPs, but at the same time we are small enough to be nimble," Barcus said. "For example, our average investment size is typically between $5 to $10 million. Some might get higher, maybe as high as $20 million over the course of a few months. But we are not like a big public pension that has to put $200 million in a fund to have it make sense. We have a very broad manager universe because of that."

Amy Jensen, who leads all investments, including direct deals in private equity, real estate and debt for the Northwest Area Foundation, credits the $420 million asset base with an ability to focus on getting a handful of quality investments each year.

It takes time to build high quality private investment allocations," Jensen said. "...Obviously, there is a tremendous amount of due diligence and a tremendous amount of work that goes into making those investments. Going to back to our size, I am fortunate that I don't have to find a lot of funds or opportunities to satisfy our allocation. If I find one or two great private equity investments a year, that's sufficient in a portfolio of our size. We tend to make fewer, larger bets to make it manageable for a staff of one. That has worked for us."

People

As discussed previously, it's the human element of the industry that determines success and failure. As institutional finance wades increasingly further into private market investments and the various structures in which these come --- the typical 10-year lock up and "2-and-20" fund, direct investments, co-investments, joint ventures, co-mingled funds, etc --- it is increasingly important to find the right people. Overwhelmingly, interviewees stated a need for a strong partnership with individuals with sound judgement and premised on aligned interests.

For Renee Hanna, director of investments at Baylor University Endowment, the starting point is proving institutional quality, which she defines as "integrity, transparency, high level of fiduciary responsibility and institutional quality valuation policies."

Next she and her colleagues vet the team.

"We like to see teams that have a history and continuity together and have a well-defined strategy with a fund that is sized appropriately for the opportunity. More quantitative analysis regarding realizations, hold periods, return attribution, etc. is also reviewed."

She stresses something that was repeated many times throughout these interviews: that private market investments typically last around a decade, and to make an investment is to hitch yourself to that manager for that ten-year period.

"At Baylor, we equally weight the quantitative aspects with the qualitative characteristics of the firm," Hanna said. "Private investments are a long-term commitment, and we want to align ourselves with teams that represent the mission of Baylor University."

Amy Jensen recalls her former boss and Bowdoin chief investment officer putting it more plainly:

"Paula Volent once said to me, 'You can't just date this manager, you're going to have to marry them.' When you invest in a private fund, that's a long-term relationship. You're going to have to be with them through the good and bad."

The qualities of what one investor looks for in an investment manager, much like what one looks for in a companion, differs from person to person. For Jensen, it's about the manager's nimbleness and foresight of future market conditions.

"I prefer to work with managers that are really thoughtful about how markets are changing and how that will impact their strategies," she said. "I work with a manager that I respect deeply because of their honesty about how the ways they made money in the past are no longer available, they are always thinking about how opportunities are shifting and where they will need to be in two years, five years and 10 years. I think that will be more important going forward than it has been in the past as more and more institutional money has flowed into the strategies that performed well over the last 10 years."

Rodney Overcash, investment director at the Cargill Philanthropies, looks for managers with something to prove. "...When trying to find a manager that stands out, it might come down to trying to find some sort of chip on their shoulder," he said. "What's the key motivational factor that's going to keep them up at night and drive them to try to be better than everybody else? We could go with a ton of groups that are going to be in similar solid trades, perform well and they'll be just fine. But what is going to drive them to be better than the others? Perhaps it's some sort of personal, emotional, motivational factor that's interesting to draw out of a portfolio manager or a team. I think that's one specific unique aspect that we try to look for."

These type of people, Overcash said, don't need to be geniuses or proficient in many areas, as long as they are an expert in the given strategy. "They don't need to have the best trading background or value investing background, but they have a great sense of prioritization. It seems like the success of the great, standout managers can be attributable to how they might size a position or how much time they might spend on it or where they might put it on their priority list. If a manager can quickly and efficiently see an opportunity, move it up and down on the priority list for potential inclusion into the portfolio, then it seems to drive the performance of their portfolio."

For Dean Duchak of the Kaiser Family Foundation, it's all about building an equal partnership and ensuring the manager doesn't see the foundation as merely another source of capital.

"One of the things that we like to focus on is 'how can our capital not just be a commodity to a manager?'" said Duchak, the firm's director of investments. "We really want this to be the true definition of a partnership, and that's often what we're looking for. Not only how they can manage and make money for us (which we obviously hope that's an outcome), but how they can be beneficial to our portfolio in other ways, and how we can be beneficial to them. Something that we like to focus on a lot is this concept of a true partnership and our capital not as a commodity, but as a relationship builder between a manager and ourselves."

Finding those types of relationships is not easy, particularly for name brand managers which often hold much of the bargaining power. That's why Duchak looks at firms earlier in their lifecycle with the potential of being partners for many years and many funds to come.

"...It's really trying to identify early on what these people are trying to build," he said. "How can we be added to them? Being transparent and upfront with them about a variety of things, including the expectation of a two-way partnership. If they're launching a fund, about their terms, their structure, their strategy, what we would expect as an LP and really trying to just continually cultivate relationships and that hopefully leads to something. I think it's an honesty and transparency idea, and also a communication thing as well."

Colin Ambrose stresses the importance of intelligence coupled with ethics. "In private investing you are committing for ten-plus years and don't have the flexibility to change your mind," he said. "It is critical to partner with high-integrity people who respect their LPs and whose terms reflect a true alignment of interest with their investors."

Ambrose said the ideal private market manager will be specialized and experienced in executing a value-add strategy. The process for doing so starts with getting to know the team.

"We spend a lot of time with the team, trying to understand their investment philosophy, culture of risk taking and whether their process is repeatable," he said. "We partner with managers who are intellectually honest, humble and continuously looking to learn and improve. We avoid managers with excess hubris who have rigid mindsets."

Diligencing an investment manager is a vigorous process. Linda Calnan, senior investment officer at the Houston Firefighters' Relief and Retirement Fund, first considers the investment manager's portfolio fit, performance, risks among the organization, team and partnership economics. But in the end, it all comes down to looking for great, not good, partners.

"We are looking for an organization that demonstrates cohesion and sound governance across the team, the organization, process vis-à-vis strategy, its relationship with limited partners, its relationship with regulators and other third-parties and in the partnership documents," Calnan said. "While we believe these factors will lend themselves well to a good partnership, we are ultimately looking for great partners that treat us as such."

The Washington University Investment Management Company utilizes both generalist and specialist managers, all of which are expected to be highly adept. "All managers need to be experts in pursuing their mandates and in being differentiated in terms of having an edge," said Kim Walker, former chief investment officer. Walker left the university endowment in December 2016.

Or as Alameda County CIO put it Betty Tse put it: "A good manager also knows how to make decisive and sound judgments based on strong fundamentals. They're not just out there to collect assets."

Edge

With near-infinite capital yet finite investment options, it's imperative that institutions seek diversification. Many might be inclined to think of diversification as the holding of various uncorrelated asset classes and not to apply that term further. However, institutions, in an effort to generate alpha, seek investment managers with an edge in the market. While the concept is common sense, how investors define it varies broadly.

"Fundamentally, you're looking for this very hard-to-define edge that a manager has," said UVIMCO Chief Investment Officer Lawrence Kochard. "In a very competitive investing environment, they have some unique way of processing information, or adding value at the company level that is better than anyone else. Oftentimes, that's really hard to achieve."

One fundamental example is Betty Tse's requirement for managers investing in a particular geography to be experts that actively scout the locale.

"...If a manager has the pulse of the quality small-cap companies it covers on their fingertips, they will be able to capture the heartbeat of these companies," said Tse, chief investment officer at Alameda County Employees Retirement Association. "These investment managers usually are in the trenches, with their feet on the ground. They know where to find the yet-to-be discovered small-cap companies."

Mary Cahill has the same "feet on the ground" preference for Emory's managers, but that edge also comes from propensity for small firms with niche strategies.

"We're seeking strong talent with a competitive advantage," she said. "...If we are investing in India, we prefer the manager be located in India. We tend to invest in more boutiquey type managers. When we invest with larger managers, we are looking for managers with a global reach and array of offerings that can supplement our own allocation research.

David Barcus said an edge can come in many different forms. "For some, this can be driven by their investment process: do they have a very process-oriented approach? Does this process create a repeatable strategy? Other times this could come from their background: where did they learn the ropes? For example, if they're investing in health care, were they previously medical doctors? Do they have that expertise? Or if they are investing in distress, do they have a legal background?"

Bob Jacksha looks to private markets for alpha or exotic beta. "Some people argue there isn't that much alpha, and I go, "That's fine." Maybe it's an exotic beta that differs a lot from what happens in the public market. That's more what we look at. Both of those are in limited supply."

At roughly $11 billion in assets, Bob Jacksha says New Mexico ERB is also in the goldilocks zone, which allows them to invest in these targeted players. "As a smaller fund, we can access some managers that are in those niche strategies, that have limited capacity of a $250 million fund that some of our large brethren wouldn't even bother with. That might offer some additional returns or a better risk-return profile than some of the large buyout funds in private equity versus a smaller strategy. A lot of times in private markets managers, we're looking for that demonstrated ability to execute in a smaller part of the markets."

A propensity for niche managers begs the question: Does "small manager" mean one that is early in its lifecycle? For Stuart Mason, the answer is not necessarily.

"While we have done some first-time funds that have GPs that we have known for some time and have confidence in or have invested previously with, we would much prefer to invest in a fund that is sized appropriately for the opportunity, and with a manager that has a history and has sponsored funds before," he said. "We basically look for the same thing in every private fund manager: a meaningful enough history of consistently addressing an asset class that we have determined is an attractive market."

Mason and his staff invest thematically. In venture, Mason seeks managers addressing data analytics, enterprise moving to mobile platforms, consumer marketplace solutions, SaaS and AI or machine learning. "If it isn't in these sectors, we probably aren't interested," he said. Those criteria narrow the field to "a relatively modest number of fund managers who are 30 or 40 something years old, who have been doing this long enough to have developed a reference network in an industry segment and an investment record that indicates success."

That thematic approach is replicated within each asset class at the endowment. "If you can pick a couple of funds that do that well, they may have a tailwind for a decade," Mason said.

Many institutions are, however, actively targeting newer managers over more established firms.

When Mercy Health's investment office wanted to take advantage of illiquidity in the high-yield market, it seeded a high-yield dislocation fund to reap both the market opportunity and the success of the fund.

While we invest with well-known, well-established managers, we are not shy of investing with boutique firms or unique opportunities," said Lela Prodani, senior investment analyst. "We engage in partnerships that might be more beneficial for us."

Lawrence Kochard has a strong portfolio, which has led the team to focus on pruning existing strategies and slowly replacing them with newer institutions.

"Meaning they're smaller, they have a longer career ahead of them and they may be operating in a better opportunity set," Kochard said. "It's hard to characterize that there's this one silver bullet, or formula that we'll look at. It's making sure that there's skill, and then making sure that the incentives are aligned so when that skill is exploited, that we get compensated appropriately."

The Conrad N. Hilton Foundation is shifting its portfolio toward smaller, newer firms. Co-Chief Investment Officer Michael Buchman said, "We think that those managers are "hungrier," more performance-driven and provide a long runway for us to partner with them."

And much like Mercy, the Foundation's search for new managers isn't relegated to only investing in funds themselves. "We will look at any opportunity and are actively working to source new relationships," Buchman said. "We've invested in first-time private funds, day-one hedge fund launches and acted as a significant investor for existing, but much smaller funds.

What's most important, he said, is ensuring alignment of interests through strong partnerships. "This approach aligns itself to partner with managers that are young and hungry. With smaller assets under management, they aren't going to get rich off management fees and are motivated by carried interest and incentive fees. By investing earlier on, it allows us to establish a relationship with that manager and to develop a true working relationship with them that only grows and strengthens over time. We seek to form true partnerships with our managers and engage them in discussions about, not only their investments, but also how they manage their business and its growth."

David Barcus sees new managers and established managers as different tools to achieve specific ends. "In certain cases, it's great to be with a growing manager, one who is eager to create wealth," Barcus said. "In other cases, it's not so bad to have an investment with a very established manager especially in a strategy where capital preservation is the focus."

No matter the stage of life in which the manager resides, Barcus stresses the need for partnership. "...Ultimately, I think the most important quality in a fund manager is their integrity and the relationship and trust that we can develop with them," he said. "Are we treated like a partner? Or are we treated like a client, another revenue stream? We're really looking to be a partner with these investors, hopefully for a very long time.

The University of Rochester investment office isn't necessarily looking for brand new managers, which often must endure growing pains, said Steve Groves, an endowment investment officer. The endowment also doesn't want a fund that has grown too large.

"We're typically looking for the sweet spot of talented managers..." said Groves. "...You can find talented teams or even a talented individual who spins out of another firm, and they've got a great track record, but they may not have the experience managing an organization, pulling a team together and overseeing a group like that without the broader organizational support that they previously had around them."

"Most importantly, it's a people business," he said. "We seek experienced managers with a strong track record, who have worked together as a team for some time. We're obviously writing large checks, so they must have the highest integrity and strong references."

Asher Noor, chief investment officer of AlTouq Group, a single-family office based in Saudi Arabia, wants access to any hard metrics that help prove a firm's track record. "More crucial, however, is discovering their commitment and ability to let the relationship blossom over an extended period of time, instead of pushing us into a business relationship from meeting number one. In the part of the world I live in, it's all based around personal relationships before the business relationships happen. It's not about going on holiday together. It's about knowing each other's successes and failures, desires and vision and the passion to build a mutually productive and lasting relationship."

Or as Yup Kim succinctly summarizes: "Integrity and the spirit of partnership – I think it's increasingly clear who views us strategically and treats us as real partners. I appreciate managers who exhibit humility and emphasize alignment."

Part IV
CHALLENGES AND TRENDS

"No matter how much experience you have, no matter how much you've seen, markets are always different. That's what makes this job endlessly stimulating and endlessly fun. That's also what's difficult," said Kathryn Crecelius, former chief investment officer of Johns Hopkins University.

Market conditions constantly change, and so do expected returns. In recent years, investors have faced significant headwinds for generating sustainable long-term returns while meeting near-term payout requirements. Ultra-low interest rates, rich valuations, geopolitical trends in the U.S. and Europe, and the unknown side effects of post-financial crisis monetary and regulatory policies produced market conditions unlike any seen previously.

Kim Walker, former chief investment officer at Washington University Investment Management Company, said a general surplus of capital is making markets crowded and inflating asset valuations. "Capital is a commodity, and it can distort fundamental valuations for some period of time and can also crowd out allocations to managers," Walker said.

So what are institutional investors doing to adapt to the market environment and fulfill their fiduciary responsibilities? To begin to answer this question, you must first understand the prevailing portfolio model adopted by much of the industry and its impact on markets. That naturally transitions to a debate over the value of certain strategies and the compensation and alignment of interests therein -- particularly within more opaque private market strategies. Then the discussion turns to the merits of active versus passive management. In summation, the result is a tactical shift in institutional investment strategy.

12. The "Endowment Model" Movement

In the 1980s, a typical public pension fund could invest all its assets in the U.S. 10-year Treasury notes, sit back and meet its expected rate of return. Markets have changed, forcing broader diversification among asset classes and investment vehicles. In the 1980s, the Yale University endowment adopted and popularized a model splitting the portfolio into six roughly equally weighted asset classes and utilizing illiquid private markets. This became known as "the endowment model." Over time, it has achieved near ubiquity among investment offices managing more than $1 billion, with most portfolios significantly exposed to alternative assets in search of uncorrelated, alpha-producing investments.

"We've seen funds moving in more diversification and alternative investments," said Bob Jacksha, chief investment officer of New Mexico Educational Retirement Board (ERB). When Jacksha joined New Mexico ERB in January 2007, the pension fund had 70 percent of assets invested in public equity, mostly in the U.S. market. Fast forward to 2016, the target allocation of public equity was lowered to 35 percent. Jacksha replaced half of the old allocation in public equity with alternative assets, which have helped battle volatility. "We realize that we do certainly give up a little bit of upside in the real strong bull markets in U.S. stocks, but being an underfunded pension plan, you just can't afford a big drawdown," he said.

"During my short time in the pension world, I've noticed that pensions are definitely moving toward the endowment model," said Sam Masoudi, chief investment officer of Wyoming Retirement System, a $7.5 billion pension fund. Masoudi also found it a trend that public pensions are hiring bigger and higher-skilled staffs with more attractive compensation packages than they used to. "I think that trend will continue to the benefit of the millions of people that depend on pension income," he said.

While risk tolerance and return objectives vary greatly among institutions, exposure to alternatives is utilized widely. When we asked investors -- at various types of institutions -- how their portfolios changed over the span of five to 20 years, a majority said the biggest change was a higher degree of diversification and active management.

"In a low-return environment, beta is not providing enough returns, and investors are focused on extracting alpha from their hedge funds and allocating more to private equity," said Colin Ambrose, chief investment officer of UJA-Federation Of New York, where half of the portfolio is allotted to those two strategies. "We continue to invest in private capital strategies so we can take advantage of the liquidity premium as long-term investors," Ambrose said.

Lawrence Kochard, chief investment officer and CEO of the University Of Virginia Investment Management Company (UVIMCO), said the proliferation of the investment model has led to competitive private markets. "...The challenge is as more money is allocated to private strategies, the prices that are paid by some of those private managers are going up, and we're later in the economic cycle. Now this becomes tough," he said.

Not only are existing investment offices allocating capital to these markets, but new and highly sophisticated investors have cropped up investing on behalf of wealthy individuals, hospital systems and corporations.

"The number of additional competitors has been a growing concern," Kochard said. "That makes our ability to get access to great funds that much more difficult. Not only has it been an issue, but it will continue to be an issue for us."

Elizabeth Hewitt, chief investment officer of Alfred P. Sloan Foundation, said the first-mover advantage exists in the endowment model movement. "Over time, the endowment model has become more popular, and you have seen a large increase in the number of institutions investing in private equity. People who were in that space early on got paid to be there. Today it's a crowded space, and it's not as easy. I don't think you'll get the returns that you have gotten over the past 10 or 15 years," Hewitt said. The Sloan Foundation is committed to rebuilding its private equity portfolio, but Hewitt has tempered her expectations. "We're mindful that our expected returns are not 300-over-equity -- they're closer to 200-over-equity," Hewitt said.

Stuart Mason, chief investment officer of the University of Minnesota Foundation, said for the endowment model to be successful, "the devil is in the details."

"At a very high level, the Yale model says 'use private investment vehicles to gain more portfolio diversification,' and capture the benefit from the illiquidity premium to produce higher long-term returns...The details that matter are how large is the allocation to private markets that makes sense for your specific portfolio and what kind of private investments are you able to professionally execute," he said.

Mason noted that small endowments with assets less than $1 billion are less likely to benefit from the alternative-heavy strategy than institutions controlling more capital. "For smaller endowments, generally speaking, those with a few hundred million dollars, it's not working very well. Part of the reason is that their allocations to private alternatives are relatively modest, and investment offices of those under $1 billion often don't have the depth in their staff to invest directly with managers, or often don't have the ability to gain access to the very best managers. So they resort to using fund-of-funds that are top heavy on fees. No surprise, the results are often disappointing," he said.

Fiscal years 2015 and 2016 have been particularly challenging for investors, which can be attributed to systematic market risk and manager selection. For example, consider university endowments, which earned a modest 2.1 percent in 2015, but lost 2.9 percent in 2016, according to research by the National Association of College and University Business Officers and Cambridge Associates.

Although institutions are long-term investors who shouldn't be swayed by a one-year or two-year slump, the gap between target and actual returns can be hard to digest. "When you have a 30-year investment horizon, you can't worry about storms that blow through, but you are a human being and so, you do," Christopher Ailman, chief investment officer At California State Teachers' Retirement System (CalSTRS). CalSTRS' $189 billion investment portfolio returned 4.8 percent in the fiscal year ended June 30, 2015, nearly 3 percentage points below its target of 7.5 percent.

No institution, despite the quality of underlying managers, is immune to market-wide declines. As was the case in 2016, when many of the largest public pension funds and university endowments saw returns decline, largely from real assets and public equity markets.

Those factors are coming to a head, which is driving investors to reevaluate their relationships with asset classes, investment vehicles and asset managers.

RETURNS OF 10 LARGEST UNIVERSITY ENDOWMENTS IN THE U.S.

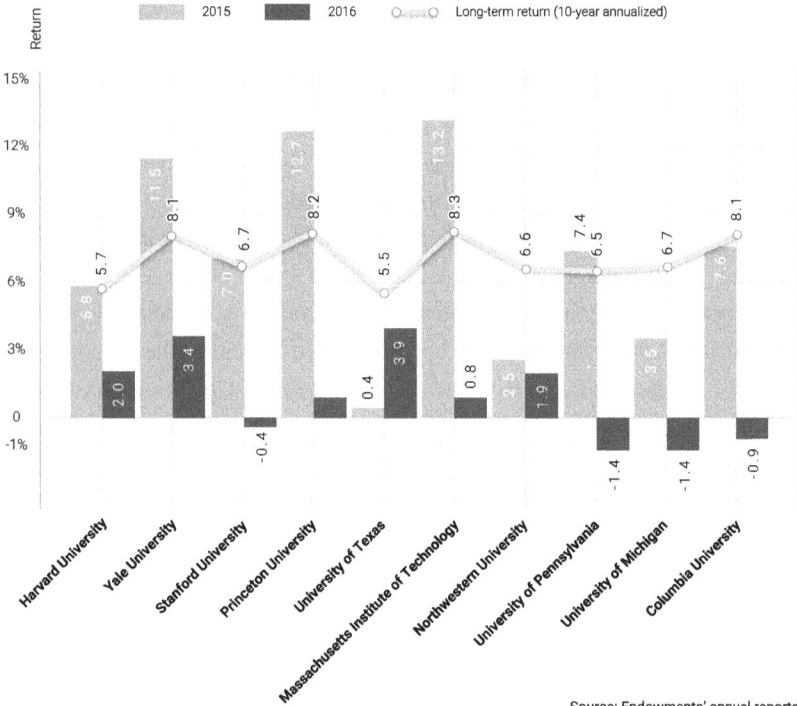

Source: Endowments' annual reports

RETURNS OF 10 LARGEST PUBLIC PENSION FUNDS IN THE U.S.

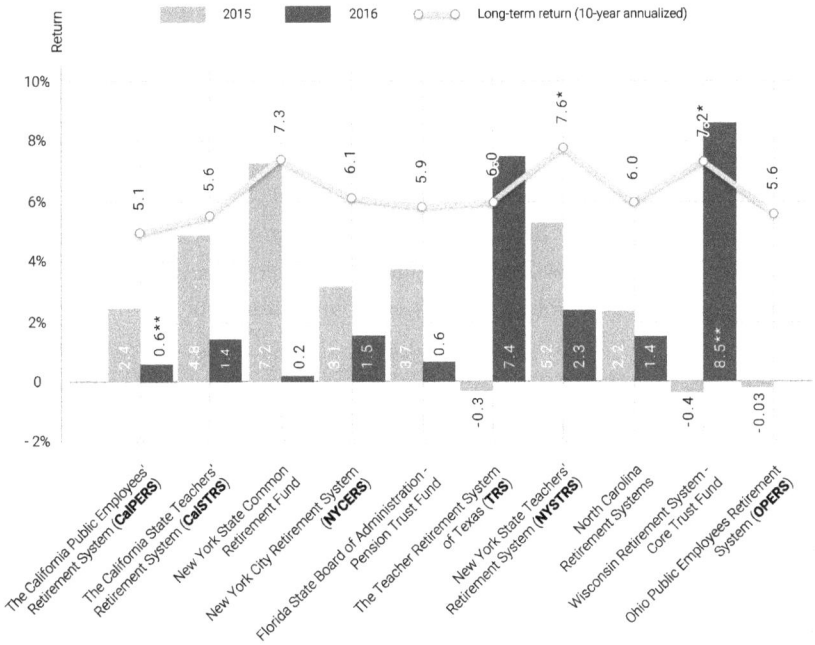

Legend: 2015 | 2016 | Long-term return (10-year annualized)

Data values shown:

Fund	2015	2016	Long-term
The California Public Employees' Retirement System (CalPERS)	2.4	0.6**	5.1
The California State Teachers' Retirement System (CalSTRS)	4.8	1.4	5.6
New York State Common Retirement Fund	7.2	0.2	7.3
New York City Retirement System (NYCERS)	3.1	1.5	6.1
Florida State Board of Administration - Pension Trust Fund	3.7	0.6	5.9
The Teacher Retirement System of Texas (TRS)	-0.3	7.4	6.0
New York State Teachers' Retirement System (NYSTRS)	5.2	2.3	7.6*
North Carolina Retirement Systems	2.2	1.4	6.0
Wisconsin Retirement System - Core Trust Fund	-0.4	8.5**	7.2*
Ohio Public Employees Retirement System (OPERS)	-0.03		5.6

* 20-year annualized return (10-year figures are not available)
** Preliminary 2016 return (actual returns are not released at the time of book publication)
Note: OPERS' 2016 return is not available at the time of book publication.   Source: Pension funds' annual reports

13. Controversy Over Management Fees

Like most things in life, high returns come with high risk and sometimes at a high cost. As an industry norm, alternative assets, or private market assets such as private equity funds and hedge funds, charge a "2 and 20" fee (2 percent of total capital committed and 20 percent of profit) for managing investments. By comparison, buying public market index funds often cost less than 1 percent of the amount invested.

When returns are strong, everyone is happy. When performance sours, as has been the case among many hedge funds, the equation breaks. As a result, asset allocators have begun to question the value of such investments and the associated fee structures. Daniel Parker, deputy chief investment officer of Texas Tech University, said, "Management fees have been allowed to become a significant driver of profits for many mature GPs and that creates an incentive misalignment. In private capital, the crystallization of carry before there are distributions, as well as the use of aggressive manager catch-ups, are likely to come under increasing scrutiny and pressure."

In recent years, the ire is most heavily directed at hedge fund managers. Over the 10-year period ending 2016, the HFRI Fund Weighted Composite Index, a benchmark index measuring hedge fund performance across sectors, returned 3.4 percent annually. Investing, instead, in the S&P 500 Index, would have returned 6.8 percent over the same period.

Floundering performance led many institutions to reduce or eliminate their hedge fund allocations. In 2014, the California Public Employee Retirement System, the largest public pension fund in the nation, announced its liquidation of $4 billion in hedge fund investments. A number of public pensions have since followed suit. In 2016 alone, the New Jersey State Investment Council cut its hedge fund allocation by half; the Illinois State Board of Investment reduced hedge fund exposure to 3 percent from 10 percent; and the New York City Employees' Retirement System announced in April the elimination of its hedge fund strategy altogether.

Some investors criticize the sentiment toward hedge funds as overreaction. "People getting upset with hedge funds is akin to someone getting upset with their insurance policy when they don't have an accident," said Baron Koch, investments director at CHRISTUS Health. "My view over the long term is that the downside protection element is still there and the long-term viability of the asset class, by and large, is still intact."

David Barcus, investment manager at Denison University, argues that high return expectations for hedge funds are not only unrealistic, but misguided. "While there has been some negative press on hedge funds and certain investors have pulled back, I personally remain a believer in hedge funds," he said. "I think calling hedge funds an asset class can be a misnomer, as they are often just investment vehicles gaining exposure to more traditional asset classes."

At Denison University, the hedge funds portfolio of the $750 million endowment is constructed around managers rather than investment types such as equity, global macro and event-driven investments. Barcus said the rationale behind this strategy is that hedge fund performance is more driven by manager skills than asset types within the funds.

He cited a 2014 study by global asset manager BlackRock to support his point. "Manager selection, as opposed to style selection, within hedge funds really drives performance. For example, performance dispersion between top- and bottom-quartile hedge funds is not reigned in when you focus on a particular strategy. Put another way, the amount of dispersion across all hedge funds in the universe is essentially the same as the amount of dispersion between funds in a particular strategy, like long/short equity or global macro.

"However, when you take the same example looking at actively managed equity mutual funds, performance dispersion is essentially halved when you compare the amount of dispersion between all funds versus the amount of dispersion between funds within a particular investment style, like large-cap growth equity funds or small-cap value funds. The message here is that the majority of dispersion in hedge funds return is driven by manager-related risks as opposed to strategy-related risks."

Barcus concluded, "Ultimately, I think we are 'net-of-fee investors.' If the net returns are attractive, and the manager is charging '2 and 20,' we won't rule it out."

Not limiting to hedge funds, it is consensus among LPs that for all private market funds to offset their high fees, manager selection is crucial. "Managers need to be able to be good enough to overcome those fees," said Lawrence Kochard of UVIMCO.

To succeed in unfavorable markets, Kochard said investors should either focus heavily on finding the best managers -- which is his strategy for the UVIMCO portfolio -- or looking for ways to reduce fees "by doing co-investing or buying secondaries at attractive prices."

The challenge, Kochard said, with the latter strategy is achieving economies of scale. "We look at co-investments, but it's hard to scale," he said. "We do a little more co-investments now than we used to, but it's not as though it'll be a large percentage of what we do. I think if you try to scale it, it would not be additive to returns."

Dhvani Shah, chief investment officer at the Illinois Municipal Retirement Fund, said that strategies like co-investments are another tool for asset allocators to use, but those too might pose new challenges in itself.

"In your typical private equity fund, with a European waterfall, you actually have a set of mechanisms for the carried interest calculations," she said. "From my perspective, the jury is out whether the new vehicles solve more problems than they create. But when it's a longer time period, such as a permanent vehicle, how is the carried interest calculated on an open-ended fund? Is it still based on divestments or on valuations over a time period? If it is the latter, the investor is still invested in the asset while the general partner is getting carried interest. Whether this alignment of interest is strong or not, really depends on the details of those vehicles. That is why I said that the jury is out because you really have to evaluate each of those strategies based on the mechanics with which some of these economics are being calculated."

JM Family Enterprises, a Florida-based automotive company, is implementing cost controls on its $1 billion retirement asset pool. Ron Virtue, the company's director of investments, said the company takes a holistic approach to balance the overall investment cost. "We constantly look at our fees and then compare to what we're getting and sometimes look at making changes as well. When we were adding a few of those past alternatives -- such as increasing emerging markets or real estate and commodities -- that could have increased our fees, we lowered fees elsewhere. For example, in U.S. large-cap, we substantially lowered our fees, so net our fees stay pretty constant," Virtue said.

"It doesn't pay to be an unsophisticated investor in alternative assets – unsophisticated investors pay more and get less in return," said Tom Masthay, director of real assets at Texas Municipal Retirement System, who is in charge of manager selection for the pension fund's real assets and real estate portfolios.

"If institutions can increase their capital flexibility and resource themselves in a manner that is focusing on net performance over horizons commensurate with liability risk, success can follow through stronger negotiating positions with investment managers and better investment opportunity and manager selection outcomes," Masthay said.

Following poor 2016 returns, hedge funds managers are being forced to change. A 2016 survey by Preqin shows that hedge funds managers found fund-raising and retaining investor capital to be significantly challenging for the year. Three quarters of the hedge funds managers surveyed are willing to reduce their fees, and many intend to spend more on marketing in 2017 in a bid to revive investor faith in hedge funds.

Dan Parker of Texas Tech University said difficult market conditions will force the asset management industry to restructure fees and filter out subpar managers. "Viable alternative fee structures going forward are likely to include a combination of lower management fees, preferred returns or hard hurdles for incentive fees/carry and the alignment of carry with distributions to LPs. Managers who are consistently able to produce alpha deserve to be compensated, but there are more pretenders than contenders," he said.

To second Parker, Neal Graziano, director of investments at the W. K. Kellogg Foundation, said the second-tier managers will eventually disappear. "There are too many hedge fund managers, and there are too many private equity managers...There are going to be those individuals that are phenomenal that are going to be able to maintain those superior economics. But that second- and third-tier is eventually going to go away" he said.

Graziano further predicted that second-tier hedge fund managers will be replaced by cheaper, artificial intelligence-powered investment tools. "On that second tier, what we've found, more specifically in the hedge fund space, is that what was alpha is just beta in sheep's clothing. With the advent of technology, we are able to map out these returns a lot better and realize that what you thought was alpha was not there, and you can get it a lot cheaper," he said.

14. Seek Alpha Or Turn Passive?

2016 was a peculiar year for institutional investors -- index funds outperformed actively managed funds; credit securities generated higher returns than equities; and the geopolitics of the U.S. election, Brexit and continued uncertainty of the European Union -- making investing ever more unpredictable and challenging for institutional investors.

"It's a difficult macro environment to navigate for an active portfolio manager," said Ana Marshall, chief investment officer of the William and Flora Hewlett Foundation.

"I would say that the biggest risks are global reflation and the European elections. The Trump Effect has just been so strong and quick. It reflects hope for U.S. growth, tax reform and spending. It's as if the market decided they wanted to price it all in at once. The biggest risk is that none of it materializes, leaving corporate profit estimates a tad too high," Marshall said.

Not only did investors reduce or terminate hedge fund commitments as mentioned earlier, but many reduced exposure to active managers. The core debate is an old and perennial one cast through the current market climate: in a richly valued, low interest rate environment, are investors better off seeking alpha at a high cost or turning to passive strategies?

Asher Noor, chief investment officer of AlTouq Group, warns that the incessant chase after alpha may hurt investors as a result of neglecting discipline. "We are always looking for the 'home run' deal. We are trying to make money out of money or putting money to good use or parking it for an unknown future. But some of the real winners in this game are the ones who have stepped off the treadmill. They are not chasing anything," he said. "It has nothing to do with their net worth or AUM. What they have achieved is the ability to curb their enthusiasm and say no, even if the economics of the deal appear juicy, but it is not something their portfolio needs. They have instilled discipline in their investment strategy. I am seeing many going too fast and too soon. Discipline within investing is not some warm, fluffy and philosophical abstract. Discipline is the key to a stable portfolio. Clearly, not everyone is giving this the due attention that it merits."

Perhaps the most worried investors of all are public pension funds. The aging population and annual payout requirements worsen the fact that most pension funds are underfunding and high costs incurred from asset managers dilutes total investment earnings when these managers fail to deliver superior returns.

"Public pensions are facing some serious headwinds -- returns are low and funding is challenged at most plans, if not all plans. Everyone is trying to find a way to protect their funds on the downside without dampening returns too much. Unfortunately, nobody seems to have found a silver bullet for the problems CIOs are facing," said Lorrie Tingle, chief investment officer of the Public Employees' Retirement System of Mississippi.

Pension funds are late adopters of the "endowment model." That limited track record of proven success has prompted pension investors (and other investors more broadly) to wonder if they would better off reverting to index-heavy allocation strategies.

Jonathan Grabel, the former chief investment officer of the Public Employees Retirement Association Of New Mexico, called alpha a "zero-sum game." "I think we spend too much time trying to achieve alpha. I think alpha is ephemeral...If we are fortunate enough to have some alpha at certain points in time, that's great, but I would much rather have a portfolio where we have the best betas and focus on things limiting our downside. That may mean sacrificing some of the upside, but I think that really helps us position our portfolio for the long term. The worst thing in the world to do is take unnecessary risks in any given market environment," he said.

In fact, some pension funds that have been sticking with passive strategies did come out of the down market unscathed. Robert Maynard, chief investment officer of the $15 billion Public Employee Retirement System of Idaho, is a firm believer in passive strategies. The portfolio takes a traditional 70/30 structure, with a majority of investments allocated in indexed index public equity funds and fixed income. Its 2016 annual report says, "The Board recognizes that passive (index fund) investing has lower costs than active investing, with regard to both management fees and transaction costs. Further, the Board also recognizes that there is uncertainty concerning whether active investing can generally outperform passive investing, particularly in the large, liquid, and efficient portions of the capital markets. Also, the Board has great confidence that a passive investment of assets in an efficient asset allocation will likely meet long-term (20 year) obligations."

But Lorrie Tingle of Mississippi PERS has a different view. While recognizing the trend of returning to passive strategies, she remains a believer in active management over the long term. "...The age-old active/passive debate rages on once again, and some plans have significantly increased their passive exposure. It's tempting when active managers struggle for a prolonged period, but we've been through those periods before. The pendulum always swings back the other way, so we're holding our current passive allocations steady," Tingle said.

15. Shifting Strategies

Putting it all together, the industry's tectonic shift toward alternatives has crowded markets, subpar performance has led to asset allocators questioning management fees and current low-growth, low-interest rate market conditions leave little room for error.

Lawrence Kochard of UVIMCO and Lorrie Tingle of Mississippi PERS both said in previous chapters that there is no silver bullet to address problems chief investment officers face today. As a result, investors are exploring new investment fronts to revive their portfolios. Some are taking advantage of new investment strategies, like direct investments and other opportunities created by post-financial crisis regulations; others hope to capitalize on demographic and economic changes in emerging markets; while certain institutions are looking beyond monetary returns to seek positive social influence through their investments.

Direct Investing And Co-Investing

Direct investing and co-investing in companies, not funds, are a rising trend among LPs. While the concept is not new, an increasing number of institutional investors are engaging in direct investing and co-investing, particularly in illiquid assets like private equity, real estate and infrastructure, since the 2008 financial crisis, a 2014 report by The World Economic Forum said. A 2015 survey of 41 large pension funds globally conducted by the Organization for Economic Co-operation and Development (OECD) shows that direct investment is currently the most common method for funds to gain exposure amongst large funds that have the size and expertise for doing so.

Missouri Local Government Employees Retirement System entered their first co-investment deal in 2010. Megan Loehner, investment director at the pension fund, recalled that they were one of the few investors in the deal back then, and today they have 10 to 15 co-investors to split any given deal when co-investing. "The largest continuing trend I've seen is co-investments," she said.

Ascension Investment Management, a $32 billion hospital investment office, is increasing commitments in direct secondary investments in portfolio companies, particularly late-stage companies that need to see an exit, within its private equity portfolio. "We think that there's an opportunity to still pick up some very good companies that are in the later stages. We've been spending a fair bit of our time looking at some of those opportunities," said Dale Hunt, Ascension's managing director of private equity.

Among different types of institutions, family offices are early adopters of these investment vehicles due to family offices' relatively simple organizational structure, which allows for autonomy over strategic changes. "An increasing number of family offices are looking for opportunities to invest directly in underlying operating companies, certainly as co-investors alongside traditional private equity sponsors and increasingly as the lead sponsor of an investment themselves," said Jed Johnson, senior managing director of private markets at Crow Holdings Capital – Investment Partners.

Capricorn Investment Group, an investment arm of entrepreneur Jeff Skoll's family office, while structuring its portfolio on a typical "endowment model," is highly active in sourcing direct deals in frontier technologies. Capricorn is an investor behind Tesla and SpaceX. Most recently, the firm invested in Planet Labs, a mini-satellites, or nanosatellites, manufacturer based in San Francisco, California. Alan Chang, a partner at Capricorn who manages the firm's venture capital portfolio, said investing in innovative companies like Planet Labs isn't just part of the firm's long-term investment strategy, but more important, fulfills the firm's mission at a higher level.

"We like complex engineering problems that may at first be a stretch and feel too ambitious, but may end up solving some of the world's biggest problems... because we are part of the Jeff Skoll group of companies and we follow Jeff's visionary idea of wanting all of us to live in a world of peace and sustainability, there's a real focus on investing on a sustainable basis," Chang said.

Capricorn, Chang said, often goes a step even further and does what he calls "reverse co-investments," where "we find the opportunities and then we bring them to some of the funds that we are invested in."

However, managing direct investments and co-investment require more manpower and oversight from LPs. Johnson warns that investors need to fairly assess their resources before following the crowd. "Some family offices are very well equipped to do that successfully. I think there are others that perhaps underestimate how competitive the marketplace is and how challenging it can be to source high quality investments and manage those companies post-closing through good and bad times," he said. "It's definitely a trend, but I do think there's a minority of family offices that have really invested in the resources to be able to execute that model successfully."

In essence, in the case of direct investment or co-investment, LPs are doing the same job as GPs -- managing portfolio companies. In other words, LPs are competing with GPs -- who have more experience and resources -- in this field. "There are about 2,000 growth equity and buyout firms in the U.S. alone. In general, those firms are staffed with highly-trained professionals who command significant compensation," Johnson said.

Craig Robbins, senior investment strategist at the Children's Hospitals and Clinics of Minnesota, warns that adopting an investment vehicle just because it's trendy won't guarantee success. "Like many trends, if you aren't on the lead or have a unique advantage, you tend to get dragged into the market and it isn't as good as an investment opportunity as you initially think," he said. "Because it's an older trend that started a number of years ago, we have to be careful that we're just not becoming another 'me too' investor."

But once LPs overcome the disadvantage of talent attraction and experience, they may have a strong edge in helping the underlying companies grow, particularly for family offices. Johnson said, "Family offices that are prepared to invest in those types of resources and teams can be competitive, because they can layer those capabilities on top of their unique perspective into a particular industry as a family office who has perhaps created their wealth in an operating business. They can layer those capabilities onto a network that's differentiated in the marketplace. But I think it takes making those real and significant investments in people and process and systems in order to be competitive.

Stuart Mason of University of Minnesota Foundation said it's crucial to be open-minded yet risk-aware when implementing new investment tools. And perhaps the most important factor is timing. "History has produced many examples where early adopters have reaped the greatest benefit. Of course new ideas or trends need to be properly vetted, but I can think of examples of timber in the 1990s, technology venture in the past decade, re-insurance and many others," he said.

Opportunities post 2008

In the wake of the 2008 financial crisis, a series of regulatory changes were introduced to the finance sector to mitigate the behavior that lead to global economic collapse. Most notably, the Dodd-Frank Wall Street Reform and Consumer Protection Act, or more commonly referred to as the Dodd-Frank, which was passed in 2010, has significantly increased government supervision on banks. For example, the Act raises reserve requirements for banks and tightens regulatory compliance for banks before issuing loans.

While the Act was intended to limit risks for large banks and companies that were once deemed "too big to fail," studies show that small banks are in fact more negatively affected by the Act. A 2015 study by Harvard Kennedy School of Government shows that community banks' market share of U.S. commercial banking assets declined twice as fast following the passage of Dodd-Frank as before, particularly in small business lending space.

Many small banks find it expensive to meet regulatory compliance under the new legislation and therefore backed out from businesses that were once profitable. "...Because of Dodd-Frank, banks have had to pull back. They no longer can provide capital to investors and investment opportunities around the world like they used to," said Eric Kirsch, global chief investment officer at Aflac.

The retreat of banks frees opportunities for market competition for institutional investors, especially deep-pocketed ones that seek diversification for their portfolios and better risk-adjusted returns.

The University of Minnesota Foundation, led by Stuart Mason, allocates half to two-thirds of its fixed-income book to "where banks don't go" strategies aiming at mid-teen percent returns. "The capital requirements for banks no longer allow them to do this certain kind of subprime lending or certain types of non-investment grade corporate lending. That creates opportunities to create higher-yielding portfolios with a managed risk profile. Banks have also largely exited the real estate lending business, which creates other opportunities," Mason said.

Kirsch identifies two areas that are particularly attractive: infrastructure and middle-market lending. He illustrates the idea with the example of road construction. "Infrastructure investments have received significant attention over the last eight or nine years. There's infrastructure debt and there's infrastructure equity. A simple example of infrastructure, building a toll road in Illinois or in the middle of Europe. Governments no longer have the money, the will power and the knowledge to build that out and maintain it, but they can, in essence, issue debt and have others do it for them."

Kirsch believes the long-term nature of such infrastructure projects align well with the objectives of long-term investors. "...The appeal of that [toll road project] is, if you're funding debt that funds an infrastructure project, that toll road is going to be around for 100 years, and it's going to collect tolls. It's going to self-fund. It's highly collateralized, but you probably need to make a 30-year investment. It's not a short-term investment," he said.

"Insurance companies have long-term views. They don't have to worry about short-term volatility and total return. That's an area where banks had been contributing capital, and they've had to pull back. Insurers are taking up that space. And I'm just using a toll road example, but this could be utility lines, wind and alternative power generation -- lots of different things."

Middle-market lending, Kirsch said, can be a highly attractive area for cash-rich investors like insurance companies. "We have a $100 billion balance sheet, so we are looking at diversifying our asset base...There are tens of thousands of small- to mid-size companies across that United States. That's the engine of our growth actually. Companies with EBITDA of $10 million to $50 million to $200 million are not necessarily public. They're privately run companies, typically a niche in their industry and have been around for 10, 20 or 30 years. They, too, need debt to finance themselves, redo a warehouse, expand operations. There's always been this whole market of middle-market lending, a whole host of lenders across the United States.

"Historically, the banks were the provider of capital to those lenders as well as the entities that disintermediated the risk. After the lenders would make the loans, they would also find buyers for the loans. The banks can no longer afford to do that business. It's too capital-intensive under Dodd-Frank. So we are stepping in, along with other insurance companies because we consider credit underwriting a core competency. Credit is something we can analyze; we can get covenants and protections. We can ride out economic cycles. That's another asset class for which we are filling a void because of our long-term nature to investments...I see the amount of incoming calls to us as an industry increasing and the amount of new things we may do versus what we might have done 10, 15 years ago increasing because banks have left the space, and we're the natural providers of that capital," Kirsch said.

Rodney Overcash, investment director at Margaret A. Cargill Philanthropies, also sees middle-market lending as a promising area, although he said the foundation hasn't coordinated a targeted strategy in the space yet. "[Regulatory changes are] making us think about how we might see some things in the debt space, where banks aren't lending as much, particularly some of the larger middle-market private equity-sponsored deals where the OCC and some of the other regulatory groups are pushing the mandate of caps on leverage for some of these big LBO deals," he said.

Investing in credit, as with every other asset class, requires good timing and strong asset managers. "Selective investments in credits trading at distressed or stressed levels could provide solid risk-adjusted returns provided the upfront credit analysis is accurate," said Jude Perez of the New Mexico Public Employees Retirement Association. "Inflation-linked strategies, such as MLPs, are offering attractive yields, but are trading in tandem with energy prices to a much greater degree than is warranted by the fundamental characteristics of the structure, so that makes it difficult."

Some investors argue that it's too early for credit to produce consistent and solid returns. "In the credit space, it's early right now, but I do think there will be an opportunity there. If you can identify the right managers who can take advantage of the illiquidity in credit markets caused by some of the regulatory changes, I think you could end up generating a decent return," Elizabeth Hewitt of Alfred P. Sloan Foundation said in an April 2016 interview.

Mark Newcomb of Washington University Investment Management Company thinks credit is overpriced, for now. "Credit will be a great opportunity in the near future. Today, we don't think credit is necessarily anything extraordinary... We see a lot of capital chasing credits right now. It doesn't really relate to the underlying fundamentals, so we find a lot of credit market to be expensive. In general, fixed income is less liquid than it was five years ago. That's a structural change, so there might be a premium that will always be there due to the structure of fixed income markets, which include credits, but it's not cyclical," Newcomb said in a July 2016 interview.

Emerging markets

Whether it's managed funds or direct investments, emerging markets have been an area of opportunity for many institutional investors. Developing economies, such as China and India, and emerging countries in Asia and South America have seen drastic social change and tremendous economic growth. And yet, the capital markets in these countries are not as mature and saturated as that of America. For investors, this can mean fairly valued or undervalued assets in economies that are supported by economic growth and demographic changes -- if you know where to look.

"In the current market, there are relatively few assets that are inexpensive, but there are pockets of value in master limited partnerships, which have arguably been oversold, and in emerging markets, especially parts of Asia, where low pricing is out of sync with above average economic growth. Investments that are uncorrelated to the richly valued public markets can be found in niche markets," Andrew Eberhart, chief investment officer of a prestigious single-family office.

"There's a deeper focus and recognition on the importance of building strong investment exposures outside of the U.S. and Western Europe," Yup Kim of Alaska Permanent Fund Corporation said.

"The long-term alpha opportunity sets in emerging markets is very compelling," said Sean Feng, an investment director at Kresge Foundation. Feng, who was born and raised in China before moving to the U.S. in 1996, has a deep understanding of the changes the developing world is undergoing. "The world we are in today is fundamentally different from 15 years ago. Today, driven by industrialization and urbanization, emerging markets comprise at least half of the global output, global growth, global fixed investment and global commodity consumption. The locus of global economic activity and dynamism has been shifting to emerging markets. In another 10 years, it is reasonable to expect that almost half of the world's largest companies could be headquartered in emerging markets," he said. "If so, the composition of global financial assets would change significantly, and global investors would have a much higher allocation to emerging markets. Such a big shift could create many potential alpha opportunities. Constructing the right team and portfolio to take advantage of such a long-term shift represents, in my opinion, one of the best investment opportunities."

Even in times when returns weren't so attractive, like in recent years where emerging stocks and local currency bonds have underperformed developed peers, many investors remain hopeful of the long-term prospect of emerging markets, largely backed by the strong potential of the consumer sector. Alan Chang, partner and managing director of Capricorn Investment Group, is one of the optimists. "We believe that in the long run, we'll see an emerging class of middle class consumers in a number of the emerging markets. You are already seeing that in China. And you are hearing a lot about that in India. Taking into account all these things, we remain very committed to the emerging markets in the long run. We think things will go better," he said.

Chang noted that it's crucial to identify "sustainable" investments. "We also believe that we have to approach it in a sustainable manner. After all, if you consider the carbon footprint of an average American versus the carbon footprint of someone living in China or someone living in India, and then think of how economically these countries will grow and that people will consume more. Clearly, there is not enough of a resource base in the world to accommodate this type of growth over time," he said.

Novisi Nirschl, director of private investments at Memorial Sloan-Kettering Cancer Center, is bullish in China, in particular. "Emerging markets are tricky these days, but in my opinion, China is still going to become the dominant economy in the mid-term. So China is still a very active spot for us as well," Nirschl said.

Stuart Mason of The University Of Minnesota Foundation said investors should prepare early for these opportunities. "I think traveling globally early in one's career to gain perspective beyond the borders of U.S. investing is also important. Spend time in China, India and Brazil. These are booming economies where you are going to encounter really interesting investment opportunities. You need to understand what's going on the ground sooner rather than later if you're going to be able to diversify the portfolio beyond the borders of just a Russell 3000 Index Fund," he said.

While countries and regions that fit the definition of emerging markets share some characteristics in terms of the degree of industrialization and urbanization, each economy and culture has nuances and subtleties that require extensive research into the underlying themes driving growth.

"I think most geographies and industries have their share of asymmetric, niche pockets of growth," Yup Kim said.

Investing in emerging markets is much about investing in the future. Therefore, many LPs take an interest in early-stage companies, budding industries and, of course, countries that are rapidly industrializing.

Alaska Permanent Fund Corporation favors two countries and two sectors in particular. "We're taking a long-term overweight view in India and Brazil, driven both by the demographic growth and consumption basket upgrade story...While certain technology and life sciences companies command rich valuations in the public markets, we continue to selectively invest in these areas on an earlier stage basis," the $55 billion sovereign wealth fund's senior portfolio manager Yup Kim said.

Kaiser Family Foundation, a Menlo Park, California-based private foundation, takes a special interest in the Indian technology sector, mostly early-stage, private market opportunities. Dean Duchak, the foundation's director of investments, said the prospect of these investments over the next five to 10 years can't be overestimated. "You look at the demographics and the consumer in India, and it's hard not to get excited about the long-term potential," he said. "India is the second most populous country in the world with more than a billion people. With the advent of the smartphone and the continued adoption amongst its people, internet penetration is rapidly increasing – and reaching people across the country. This new mode of mobile connectivity, e-commerce and derivatives of e-commerce (infrastructure, logistics, finance etc.) present an incredible greenfield opportunity, given the absolute scale of the country. So in summary, it's the scale of the country and the way by which its people are consuming."

The University of Minnesota Foundation focuses on a set of specific targets within China. Chief Investment Officer Stuart Mason said, "When we go into a different country like China, we have a very narrowly prescribed set of trends that we think are current opportunities in China. We would try to find managers who are investing in those. For example, there are more consumer-service related venture and private equity opportunities that we would purse in China. There are certain niches in real estate in China, or in Asia generally, that we think are currently attractive. In Brazil or India, we'd have a different strategy in those geographies."

Robert C. Lee, former director of hedge funds at the Employees' Retirement System of Texas, is bullish on Asia broadly. "There is a lot to be done in Asia right now, generally because the risk appetite is lower these days. I think a lot of people have started to pull out of some markets prematurely, and it has created quite a bit of opportunity," he said.

Feng said while investors look to increase capital exposure to emerging markets to take advantage of the rapid growth, implementation might take longer and be difficult. He said there are five reasons for this: "historical high emerging market volatility (perceived as higher portfolio risk and career risk), challenge of finding managers who can consistently generate alpha, benchmark risk, home country-bias and resource constraints."

"The diversity within EM and the rapid changes within each EM country, in my opinion, require a different investment approach – a more selective (regarding which country to invest) and more focused (on niche opportunities) approach," he said.

Take health care sector as an example. Health care in the U.S. is a developed and saturated market. Health care is expensive while demand continues to grow due to an aging population. By comparison, in developing countries, health care infrastructure is often inchoate and consumption is much weaker. "In 2012, per capita health care spending in India and China was about $60 and $320, compared to $4,600 and $8,900 for OECD and the U.S. India and China's total health care spending are about 4 percent and 5 percent of their total GDP, compared to 18 percent in the U.S.," Feng said.

"In health care, we see most opportunities residing in the U.S., China and India. Opportunities in the U.S. health care sector are driven by an aging population, unsustainable health care spending and true innovation, while opportunities in emerging markets are mostly catch-up spending stories driven by a supply-and-demand mismatch," he said. "In China, total health care spending is expected to increase from $350 billion in 2011 to $1 trillion (7 percent of GDP) in 2020, resulting in double-digit growth opportunities for most health care subsectors. Such change has been creating different types of investment opportunities such as consolidation, local replacement or true global competitiveness."

Even for investors who have not invested in any emerging markets yet, it's become an area difficult to ignore. "Geopolitics in general -- things like ISIS, Russia, Ukraine, North Korea, China and the South China sea and the Chinese economy, which is a big part of the emerging markets situation -- are all issues that we think about a lot," said Bob Jacksha of the New Mexico Educational Retirement Board.

Jonathan Hook, chief investment officer of the $2.2 billion Harry and Jeanette Weinberg Foundation, is looking to increase emerging markets allocation in the Weinberg Foundation's portfolio. "We are still early in terms of building our international exposure and most of that is just timing...We have more work to do on the non-U.S. and emerging markets side, and that is where we would expect to see some long-term benefits, even if not in the short run. We think there's terrific long-term growth in other parts of the world, but it may not materialize immediately. This is an area in which we would anticipate adding exposure," Hook said in a December 2015 interview.

Since then, the Weinberg Foundation has added a few managers in Asia. Hook said they are looking to add more, particularly in Asia and ASEAN countries, before 2017 ends. "We are a bit underweight in emerging markets today, and we will likely reduce some U.S. exposure to help us add to emerging markets," he said in an April 2017 interview.

Impact Investing

In April, the $12 billion Ford Foundation announced to commit $1 billion in impact investing to "earn not only attractive financial returns but concrete social returns as well," as it said in its press release.

Ford Foundation's bold move stirred the already heated discussion around impact investing. First introduced in 2007 at a convention by The Rockefeller Foundation, the concept was derived from socially responsible investing (SRI), environmental, social and governance (ESG) and mission-related investing, as termed by many philanthropic foundations and religious-affiliated health care systems.

SRI or ESG policies often restrict the organization from investing in companies whose operations violate the organization's values. Impact investing ventures one step further to proactively seeks investment opportunities that benefit society. From our interviews, we learned that many LPs, notably foundations, health care systems and family offices, are expanding their existing SRI policies to an impact investing model.

"Mission-related investing is growing and expanding so fast...It is really hard for a mission-driven organization like a foundation to not have their mission reflected in their investment strategy," said Amy Jensen, investment director at Northwest Area Foundation, a $420 million charitable foundation based in St. Paul, Minnesota. "I would say even two years ago it seemed like it was in the early stage. Now, the number of people that are talking about it and the number of managers that are rolling out strategies show how rapidly that part of the market has developed."

In early 2014, Northwest Area Foundation made a commitment to expand its mission-related investments within its current portfolio. In other words, the foundation is looking to invest in assets aligned with the foundation's mission. This also allows Jensen, the only investment professional at the foundation, to work closely with the grant-giving side of the organization, which is uncommon for a typical foundation operation. "Historically, there has been a significant division between investments and programs at foundations...The opportunity to try and align our investments with their work, with our grantees and with our program objectives, that's really remarkable. That aspect of my job is incredibly exciting for me," Jensen said.

Ascension Investment Management manages assets for Ascension Health, a faith-based health care system whose investment guidelines are based on teachings of the Catholic Church, follows both its established SRI guidelines and the newer impact investing philosophy.

Like many Catholic institutional investors, Ascension's SRI guidelines are based on the U. S. Council of Catholic Bishops investment guidelines, which lay out specific areas they do not invest in. "Tobacco is a good example; Ascension Investment Management will not permit investments in a company that has more than 20 percent of its revenue in tobacco," said Chief Investment Officer David Erickson.

In addition to abiding by the existing SRI guidelines, Ascension is also proactively looking for investments that "not only have a good financial return, but also promote a social good." Erickson said, "We identify that as a company or project that either supports the world's poor and vulnerable or promotes good stewardship of our environment. Those two categories cover lots of things. The environment might be clean energy or clean water. The poor and vulnerable might be food, education, health care, etc."

"Through that combination of restricting investment in things that violate the teachings of the Catholic Church and investing in things that promote the teachings of the Catholic Church, we think that we are using our money as best as we can," Erickson said.

Similar to Ascension, SSM Health, a Catholic health care system with $4 billion in assets, is replacing portfolio companies that were screened out by its guidelines with new investments that promote social good.

In 2016, SSM Health blacklisted and divested from all the coal companies in its public equity portfolio, as part of Chief Investment Officer Michael Malewicz's initiative to align his investment office's goals with that of the hospital's sponsoring organization, The Franciscan Sisters of Mary. "[Our sponsoring organization] had made the decision to divest of all fossil fuel holdings some time ago, and we had been in discussions with them about how we could align our objectives better," Malewicz said.

Following the divestment, SSM Health dedicated a slice of its private equity portfolio to new opportunities within alternative energy, energy production and what Malewicz called "caring for creation" -- a broadly defined group of businesses that benefit the underserved.

Ascension's SRI guidelines list more than 800 public companies globally they deem as unsuitable for investment because their revenue is derived from things that Ascension believes violate the teachings of the Catholic Church. However, it's not always easy to draw a clear line between what fits and doesn't fit their guidelines. "As part of our guidelines, we have a philosophy section where we try to capture things that aren't necessarily in black and white. There are a lot of times where we'll come across a situation not captured in the specific guidelines, but it definitely would not be something that we think would promote Catholic teachings. For instance, it might be predatory lending, or it might be environmental, or it might be a social impact on how they're treating their workers. It's hard to put a rule-based analysis on those companies in a lot of those cases," Erickson said.

Erickson said he comes across such cases almost every quarter, if not every month. "Considerable effort goes into this process. At the end of the day, you have a portfolio that is really avoiding anything we think violates the teachings of the Catholic Church. At Ascension Investment Management, we have our investment people review the portfolio and look at the names. We think the combination of having a restricted list and then applying an overarching philosophy can help us cover those grey areas and takes us as close as we can be," he said.

Elaine Orr, former director of investments of the $7.1 billion Silicon Valley Community Foundation, encountered a similar problem. The foundation has a dedicated impact pool set up to specifically invests in environmental and social strategies, but turning this broad -- and sometimes vague -- concept into a concrete, precise objectives is a work in progress. "We wrestle with the pool's investment objective, much like I think any other asset owner in this space," Orr said. "First of all, no one has the monopoly on what is 'good' and 'best.' If I were to say I care about water, you might care about forests and someone else would be passionate about clean energy. It's challenging to wrap all that up in a coherent way into a comprehensive strategy...In the social impact pool, we continue to work with our consultants to enhance its environmental, social and governance metrics and to include public and private equity exposures. On the whole, we believe defining the impact goals and measuring the impact outcome may be more precise with illiquid exposures, rather than with a passive index approach."

Mercy Health, a Roman Catholic health care system with $2.5 billion of investable assets, also refrains from investing in tobacco companies under its social responsibility mandate. The mandate provides a list of restricted securities to

Mercy's asset managers. The investment committee is to expand the mandate to a broader scope, said Lela Prodani, senior investment analyst at the Mercy.

"These approaches could range from exclusionary screening (similar to the no-tobacco restriction that we currently have in place), to investing with managers that incorporate ESG screening in their process, to more direct approaches, like impact investing. As of right now, we plan to educate the committee about the topic and its application. Once we have a good discussion with the committee about the way Mercy wants to approach social responsibility, we are going to implement it," Prodani said.

From her experience, Prodani noted that the U.S., as a country, is lagging in impact investing. "A lot of European investors have been engaged in SRI mandates for quite some time now," she said. "I think we're a little bit behind here in the U.S, but from recent conversation with peers, more and more people are taking on socially responsible investing initiatives, especially nonprofits firms or those with an affiliation with a mission or religious order. I feel like investors want to do something more than just invest, they want to impact the community as well."

One argument critics often make against impact investing is the practice will forgo financial returns, but Prodani is unconvinced. "We have done some research in this area and don't think this is necessarily true. We think that sustainable investing can provide returns that are in line with their respective benchmarks. However, as with every manager, we think manager selection is key in this area as well," she said.

Part V
SELECTED TRUSTED INSIGHT EXCLUSIVE INTERVIEWS

An "Orthogonal" View On Venture Capital And Emerging Markets

Alan Chang, Partner and Managing Director, Capricorn Investment Group

Alan Chang is partner and managing director at Capricorn Investment Group, an investment arm of entrepreneur and former eBay president Jeff Skoll's family office. Chang is responsible for a multi-asset portfolio in Asia and other emerging markets and Capricorn's global venture portfolio.

Previously, Chang worked with early-stage venture investments at DFJ New England and was an analyst at Montgomery Securities. Chang holds a bachelor's degree from Duke university in electrical engineering, computer science and art history. He then received an MBA from Harvard Business School.

Chang was named to Trusted Insight's 2016 Top 30 LP Rising Stars In Venture Capital. He graciously spoke with Trusted Insight on January 13, 2016.

Trusted Insight: You earned a triple major from Duke: electrical engineering, computer science and art history. Not to suggest that anyone must fit into a certain box, but at face value, your studies don't seem to align with your career trajectory. How did you become interested in finance and end up at Montgomery Securities?

Alan Chang: When I was in college, I had a few internships. One of those was at JP Morgan. That's when I got some exposure to investment banking. I also worked at IBM and Intelsat, a then U.N. equivalent of satellite telecommunications provider.

The great thing about college was that it allowed me to explore all these opportunities, and as you can tell from my three majors, I have interest in many, many areas. From my internship at JP Morgan, it occurred to me that while building circuits was interesting, it was also very interesting to figure out how companies are built.

That's when I started exploring a career trajectory in investment banking, which offered me the perfect opportunity to understand how successful companies were built, how they were taken public and why, or if companies were able to build strategic value in the M&A deals I worked on while I was at Montgomery.

Trusted Insight: How did your studies in various areas help form your investment philosophy?

Alan Chang: It turns out electrical engineering and computer science are two majors that focus a lot on logic and looking at foundational parts. But where does art history fit in? Clearly, the study of fifth century Buddhist art probably doesn't fit in specifically. I think the benefit of a liberal arts education is that it teaches you how to learn. It is the conduit through which you learn how to learn, as opposed to learning something very, very specific.

On the electrical engineering and computer science side, clearly, it's about logic. Thinking in systems and thinking in components and thinking in how things fit has worked out very well in a lot of our technology investments that we've made at Capricorn.

Also on the art history side, it lends that macro lens that allows me to look at trends. In very simple words, art history was about connecting the dots. It's using different works of art at different periods and finding the connection and reading the trends between them. For example, one of the areas I focused on was fifth century Buddhist art. Buddhism was spread from India to China. Overall, the Buddhist statues were changing from a very Greco-Roman style to an Indian style and then to a much more Chinese style. It was about noticing how things change over time, mapping those and trying to find a connection and see a trend.

Art history gives that top-down approach, while electrical engineering and computer science allow for the logical thinking. This allows for building systems and very technical due diligence. These skills are still being used today.

Trusted Insight: You have spent the majority of your career at Capricorn. Anecdotally, it appears institutional investing has a relatively high turnover rate, but in your case that doesn't seem to be true. Is this a function of your personality, the company or a combination?

Alan Chang: I think it's a function of a number of things. Clearly all the things that you laid out, but the best part is that with Capricorn, we have a real focus on investing for the long run because of our structure and the nature of the capital.

It is a place I enjoy a lot, and we have an approach to allocating assets on an endowment model basis for various asset classes, but there is also the opportunity to invest into great companies directly. These include SpaceX, Tesla, Yammer, Twitter, Vitaminwater and more recent investment in nanosatellites via Planet Labs. There's a variety of opportunities to stimulate the mind. I think that's the most interesting part.

Finally, because we are part of the Jeff Skoll group of companies and we follow Jeff's visionary idea of wanting all of us to live in a world of peace and sustainability, there's a real focus on investing on a sustainable basis.

Trusted Insight: You manage Capricorn's portfolio in Asia and other emerging markets. 2016 has seen a tough start especially in markets outside of the United States. How do you maintain your desired risk-return profile for this portfolio in a market like this?

Alan Chang: It's a mix of things. We believe that in the long run, we'll see an emerging class of middle class consumers in a number of the emerging markets. You are already seeing that in China. And you are hearing a lot about that in India.

Taking all these things into account, we remain very committed to the emerging markets in the long run. We think things will go better. We also believe that we have to approach it in a sustainable manner. After all, if you consider the carbon footprint of an average American versus the carbon footprint of someone living in China or someone living in India, and then think of how economically these countries will grow and that people will consume more. Clearly, there is not enough of a resource base in the world to accommodate this type of growth over time. I think it's going to be very, very important to find a way to invest into, let's call it, the sustainable emerging consumer in these countries.

As for the year 2016 and how we are positioned, we have fortunately performed very well in 2015, but on an annual basis, we actually don't move the needle that much. Because of the nature of the capital and how we invest, we tend to focus on finding the right companies and the right managers to invest in these regions. These managers and companies have always exhibited an amazingly high degree of resilience versus the local markets, especially when the local markets are seeing volatile times.

For us, it's about finding the right managers and the right companies and sticking with them for the long run.

Trusted Insight: Your educational background seems like a perfect setup for managing a venture portfolio. What's your approach to this portfolio and how has it developed since you've taken control of it?

Alan Chang: It's a mix of really great venture fund managers as well as investments into companies directly. These include co-investments or sometimes what we call "reverse co-investment," where we find the opportunities and then we bring them to some of the funds that we are invested in.

For venture managers, it's really about finding the right people. What I've found is that we have been very lucky in having great access to proven, traditional venture managers. We've also had great success in some of the emerging managers we have backed. In a number of funds, we have been an LP since fund I, and these very successful funds have been raising funds up to fund III, IV and V now. They have done very well.

Trusted Insight: Q4 2015 was characterized by a slowdown in VC investment, but 2015 as whole was a record year for VC investment. What is your outlook for venture capital in 2016?

Alan Chang: My general thesis is that in years when there are a lot of venture funds getting raised, the returns won't be as great. But in years when everybody is worried there is less capital getting raised, sometimes the returns turn out to be better.

Looking back, some of our best-performing managers were in really terrible years, and it so happened that a number of them were raising their second funds. I believe that generally, an emerging managers' second fund, if they do it right, often turns out better than the first one, as they got their methodology honed down. A few of our great emerging managers who raised their second funds in 2008 were multiples over their Cambridge benchmark. Now, of course, 2008 was also a terrible year for raising venture capital toward the later part of the year given the global financial crisis.

Of course, investing into venture is not a game of averages. Really, the macro trend matters less to us in our daily decision-making process than who it is that we are investing with.

Trusted Insight: What geographies and sectors do you find most intriguing in venture capital?

Alan Chang: We have a little bit of a contrarian streak to us. We also -- because of the vision of helping to find investments and fund ventures that help to create a world of peace, prosperity and sustainability -- like technology or sectors that others may be very bearish about.

For example, we continue to heavily focus on clean energy. We also have a company focusing on nuclear fusion. If we want to invest in great opportunities and take advantage of the long-term nature, one technology area that may be controversial but could have a huge impact if it is successful is nuclear fusion.

Basically, we like complex engineering problems that may at first be a stretch and feel too ambitious, but may end up solving some of the world's biggest problems. In that case, many of the investments that I quoted you earlier, such as Tesla and SpaceX, are the ones that fit this criterion very well.

Trusted Insight: What trends have you identified over time in venture capital?

Alan Chang: One example would be nanosatellites. Nanosatellites, as you have seen, are represented by our investment in Planet Labs. The founders came to us after leaving NASA and said, "Hey, we can launch cell phones into space. We can take pictures with it."

On the surface, you might think, well, what can you do with this? It turns out that having frequent images for a very, very low price using consumer-style electronics would fit into a core type of disruptive technology, which is now called nanosatellites. You can see a lot of these in companies such as Spire, Planet Labs and a number of other space technologies to capture images. In the example of Planet Labs, an image of the whole world on a daily basis allows you to start tracking agricultural runoffs, deforestation, potentially human trafficking and a number of big world problems that you can start to solve.

Sometimes, though, it is a solution that a lot of consumer technology companies also need. These guys have a lot of commercial customers. In late 2012, I found the team and identified this trend. That was when we seeded the company. Now you not only see a lot of nanosatellites, but also see companies providing services through nanosatellites. Some of these companies provide small rockets or actually launch the small satellites.

You're seeing an industry transformed from the 60s when people used to build billion-dollar satellites the size of a building. Then these satellites need to be launched by big rockets, and the launch cost is ultra-expensive at hundreds of thousands of dollars per kilogram. Now, very, very small nanosatellites like Planet Labs' are just the size of a big bottle of wine. The total launch cost is exponentially lower, given the much smaller volume and mass, and these are also much cheaper to produce.

Trusted Insight: What's the number one lesson you've learned over time as an institutional investor?

Alan Chang: It's about staying curious. I think that's been one of the greatest attractions about my job at Capricorn: the variety of opportunities to get very curious about.

Sometimes it's about orthogonal thinking. In Planet Labs' case, the founders' thinking wouldn't allow them to prosper at NASA. So they decided to start a satellite/hardware company when the whole venture industry in 2011 or 2012 was focused around social media. That was when Groupon was a hot company and people were focused on flash sales, but it was important to think orthogonally and find contrarian ways of thinking. It's not staying contrarian for the sake of being contrarian, but trying to find ways to see if you can find a way to -- to borrow the Apple phrase -- "Think Different."

Also, staying mission-aligned is important. For us, it means making investments that we believe will solve the big problems in the world, but also benefit all of us financially. When you make good choices for the world, sometimes things work out financially as well. That is also a great way for one to stay passionate about work. Find a way to feel very passionate about your work, and it's a great way to wake up in the morning.

As I often describe, our mission alignment is a great way to get me up in the morning and get me excited about the day ahead. And the endowment-style portfolio allocation approach gives me the "sleep at night" insurance.

'This Is A Numbers Industry; You Are As Good As Your Numbers'

Ana Marshall, Chief Investment Officer, The William and Flora Hewlett Foundation - Part I

Ana Marshall is vice president and chief investment officer for the William and Flora Hewlett Foundation. She is responsible for the asset allocation and strategic investment policy recommendation and implementation of the $9 billion endowment portfolio. Previously, she served as a senior portfolio manager of global and emerging market equity portfolios at RCM Capital Management. Prior to RCM, Marshall worked as an portfolio manager of emerging market debt and equity portfolios at Bank of America.

Marshall began her career in 1986 as a research analyst of high-yield assets, including corporate debt, distressed debt and emerging market sovereign bonds. Marshall graduated Magna Cum Laude from the University of San Diego in economics and earned her Chartered Financial Analyst designation in 1989.

Marshall was named on Trusted Insight's 2017 Top 30 Women Chief Investment Officers. Her interview is split into two parts. In the first part, she shares her experience as a female institutional investor and why she believes men and women have equal chances to succeed in this industry despite a wide gender gap currently.

Trusted Insight: What is your experience as a female chief investment officer, considering the fact that women are underrepresented within the institution investment industry, particularly at senior levels?

Ana Marshall: I know many people view the lack of senior-level women in investments as an issue. It's never been an issue for me during my entire career. It's always been about, "can you deliver?" Luckily, unlike other industries, this is a numbers industry. You are as good as your numbers. As long as your numbers are good, you are willing to work really long hours and travel frequently, there is opportunity.

I've been here for 13 years, so my board knows me super well. However, I have heard from a few of my peers that there is an unspoken boys network that could at times undermine the CIO. That sounds like something that could be related to how a specific board functions and less about the woman in the job. Board delegation is usually an investment policy issue, and it's written regardless of whether the CIO is female or a male. It's simply conflicts arise in moments of high stress. For example, during the crisis, some people felt that is was a sexist thing when a board questions you. I would say it wasn't. It was about how you are doing, how the portfolio returns look and your relationship with the board.

Trusted Insight: What do you think the industry can do to change the situation?

Ana Marshall: I would say one of the ways is just having more female board members. That's a long-term plan. I'm starting to see more openness to having women at the board level. The investment management business is a business that requires 24-hour focus. As a CIO and as a director of an asset class, you have to be available and accessible 24/7.

I think some women and men self-select out of really senior roles. A person who's willing to work 24/7 is going to appear to be a more dependable person to promote.

Trusted Insight: Is it more of a social change that will need to happen in maintaining a balance between work and life?

Ana Marshall: These are jobs with a great deal of responsibility and for both men and women, and for both it's hard to stay balanced. I would say CIO's and senior asset class directors have more balance than investment banking, but our spouses would probably disagree there is balance in our lives. We are on planes all the time. We miss our kids' birthdays and recitals. We miss our anniversaries. We have the same trade-offs as men in these roles.

Trusted Insight: What is the most challenging aspect in your job as chief investment officer?

Ana Marshall: The most challenging aspect is keeping the investment team able to recover from a mistake made in manager selection, something bad happening in the market, being able to support them and give them the confidence that we can do things and serve as a sounding board. That is basically my job. Strategic vision and mentoring is basically what I'm there for.

Trusted Insight: How does the foundation's mission influence your approach on investments or your enjoyment of the job?

Ana Marshall: I would say it impacts the team itself or the way we hire. Every person on the team has to have some part of this foundation granting activity that they really believe in and that they're passionate about. It's a small team. We have seven investment professionals. The more we see our work is connected to a higher purpose, the better the team works.

Trusted Insight: What involvement does your governing board have in the investment decision-making process?

Ana Marshall: The board has very clear delegation of authority to the investment committee. The investment committee has delegated authority to the CIO for everything except asset allocation and benchmarking, which are typically discussed once every three to five years. Manager-specific decisions are delegated to the CIO.

Trusted Insight: How would you describe the investment strategy and team culture at Hewlett Foundation?

Ana Marshall: We have a broadly diversified portfolio with a fair use of illiquids -- very much like the Yale model. We don't tend to be very fancy. We don't do a lot of complicated derivatives. We don't do a lot of what people would call innovative strategies. Our value added is manager selection. It's really about the relationship with our managers.

Trusted Insight: Currently, what kind of managers are you looking for?

Ana Marshall: We've got a fairly mature portfolio. This means we don't have a lot of new managers in and out of the portfolio every year. These are very long-term relationships. There might be one or two new managers a year that come into the portfolio, usually on the private side. There might be another one or two on the public side. We try to keep a concentrated portfolio. So, if you're going to bring a manager in, there's usually somebody on their way out. They're usually high active risk kind of managers on the public side of it. We usually have watched managers on the private side. If they're new managers, we probably have watched them through at least two funds before getting involved.

How Hewlett Foundation Positions Portfolio For The Unpredictable Future

Ana Marshall, Chief Investment Officer, The William and Flora Hewlett Foundation - Part II

2016 was a peculiar yet interesting year for institutional investors -- index funds outperformed active equity managers; geopolitical factors such as the U.S. election, Brexit and political turbulences in European countries rattled the macroeconomic environment, making investing ever unpredictable and challenging for institutional investors.

In part two of Trusted Insight's interview with Ana Marshall, chief investment officer of the William and Flora Hewlett Foundation, Marshall discusses these topics; her outlook on return prospect and interest rates; and her strategy to guard Hewlett Foundation's portfolio against risks and uncertainties.

Trusted Insight: In your 2016 interview with us, you mentioned that benchmarks would have a hard time getting more than their 6 percent annual return in the foreseeable future until the U.S. rates start to normalize. Has your perspective changed at all?

Ana Marshall: No. In 2016, the typical 70/30 portfolio returned a bit above 6 percent and that was only after Trump was elected. Once Trump got elected, it was the concept of stimulus, tax cuts, reflation and normalization of rates that got you back up about 8 percent into year end. It's a difficult macro environment to navigate for an active portfolio manager. Last year was a year where index funds beat active equity managers. Even on the fixed income side, it was a really interesting year.

The truth is, 2016 was not a straight-line year. Now rates will start normalizing as the Fed removes accommodation. Rates typically normalize when there's growth, and growth is good for equities. If rates normalize at a pace that's been pre-told to the market, then fixed income won't do that poorly. It all kind of works out.

Trusted Insight: Currently, what risks are foundation investors facing within that macro environment?

Ana Marshall: I would say that the biggest risks are global reflation and the European elections.

The Trump Effect has just been so strong and quick. It reflects hope for U.S. growth, tax reform and spending. It's as if the market decided they wanted to price it all in at once. The biggest risk is that none of it materializes, leaving corporate profit estimates a tad too high.

Trusted Insight: How are you positioning your portfolio in order to guard against those risks?

Ana Marshall: One of the things we do is sharpen our pencils on the impact on the portfolio of a variety of macro scenarios. What parts of our portfolio will be impacted from unexpected rise in inflation, or rise in unexpected inflation more than what's being priced in? What part of our portfolio is growth, what part of our portfolio benefits from nominal growth rising? What parts of our portfolio are more sensitive if the central banks get ahead of conditions? We try to figure out this period of change and where the sensitivity lies in our portfolio.

Trusted Insight: What is your expectation for the potential interest rate rise in June? Are you optimistic?

Ana Marshall: It's funny that we now talk in terms of optimism about rising rates. I do believe that rates will be raised. I believe that there's at least two to three times this year. I think they want to see if the first one has any impact at all. The Fed raised in march and likely two more times in the fall.

Trusted Insight: Why has it been an interesting year for fixed income?

Ana Marshall: Overall, fixed income had quite a volatile year -- very similar to equities -- where they had a big disruption in the credit side in Q1 2016. Since then, there has been a compression in risk spreads in the credit side up until the election. After the election, we've had further compression. The credit market did very well last year, but it wasn't because there was a huge change in yields. Instead, the strong returns were due to a reduction in the risk premium as investors believed that there would not be a recession. The election took recession as a left tail risk off the table, so that's what got priced into the market.

Trusted Insight: Is that within private credit?

Ana Marshall: Both, private credit and public credit. Both the high yield and the private credit market. In 2016, credit outperformed equities.

Trusted Insight: In what areas do you expect to see continued growth?

Ana Marshall: It's hard to see returns in 2017 from further risk compression in credit. That said, I don't envision a sell-off in credit. Credit has the advantage of compounding cash flows at a single-digit rate of return. Equity upside is possible underpinned by improving fundamentals.

Trusted Insight: Are there other assets that you think are overvalued?

Ana Marshall: No. I actually don't see huge over valuations anywhere. I don't see huge under valuations anywhere. Things are trading more or less at full value across every asset class. We struggle to find any place in the portfolio where we say, "Wow, this is a really good deal."

Trusted Insight: What's your impression of emerging markets?

Ana Marshall: It's interesting, because emerging markets have done well so far this year. They did well at the tail end of last year. The belief was that some global growth will come back and that you have this super leverage trade on improved global growth. It's been very specific though. Idiosyncratic risk among emerging market countries is higher than it has been in a long time. Many individuals or chief investment officers don't have global emerging market mandates, and so they basically choose the countries. Picking the right countries is more important now.

If you were in Brazil or Hong Kong, you might have done fine. If you were in Mexico or Egypt, you might have done less well. I think it's going to be an interesting thing to watch people's emerging market performance relative to the benchmark in a year where active managers had a hard time beating benchmarks anyway. Your country selection in emerging markets probably had more idiosyncratic risk than ever.

Trusted Insight: We recently interviewed the CIO of a major university endowment who was fervently against the idea of benchmarking foundations. Do you agree with that?

Ana Marshall: Well, you can be fervently against benchmarking. The only way that a board of a foundation from a fiduciary position knows if assets are being taken care of is if they have a way to measure. Some boards want to measure the investment team skills at asset allocation or the skills in manager selection, and some want to measure both. Many feel they need to measure the return of the foundation against what they could go get at Vanguard with a very low cost index option of 70/30. From a fiduciary perspective, I don't see how a board member doesn't ask for it. I'm on four boards, and I ask for it.

The one area that I do not agree with is using peer benchmarks where the board holds the portfolio return up against other endowments and foundations. The reality is that every portfolio is run with a different risk tolerance that is appropriate only to the institution and that has been agreed upon by the board and the CIO. Just comparing return numbers on the surface fails to capture many other factors.

Portfolio Hedging During The Financial Crisis And Investing In Today's Market

David Erickson, Chief Investment Officer, Ascension Investment Management

David Erickson is the chief investment officer at Ascension Investment Management, where he is responsible for the administration, management and coordination of investments and operations. Prior to Ascension, he was chief investment officer at the University of Wisconsin Foundation from 2002 to 2009.

Earlier in his career, he was a vice president and investment strategist for Strong Capital Management in Wisconsin and worked for PNC Bank/PNC Capital Markets in Pennsylvania, Chemical Bank in New York and Firstar Bank in Wisconsin as a derivative specialist. Erickson holds a bachelor's degree in economics from Wheaton College. He is also a Chartered Financial Analyst.

Erickson was named on Trusted Insight's 2016 Top 30 Hospital Chief Investment Officers. He graciously spoke with us on May 16, 2016.

Trusted Insight: Your career began in investment banking. What prompted the transition into institutional investing?

David Erickson: I spent about 10 years of my career in investment banking, primarily in derivatives trading. Then in 2001, I started to have a family and wanted to move closer to my family in Madison, Wisconsin. However, it was really hard to find a derivative-focused job in that area of the country. I found my way to the University of Wisconsin Foundation as an analyst and ended up spending eight years there. By the time I left, I was the chief investment officer and had really good mentors on the investment committee. It was a really great environment for me to restart my career.

Trusted Insight: What initially attracted you to institutional investing?

David Erickson: There are a lot of similarities between derivatives trading and institutional investing. Working within derivatives was a good education because you had to know the markets. We mostly traded in fixed-income and equity derivatives, but credit derivatives were also starting to come into play. It was a multi-asset class discussion. I like thinking about markets; you're always trying to think about if equity is going up or down, where interest rates are going to go, or whether you should do interest rate swaps or not. So when I interviewed for the position at the University of Wisconsin, there were a lot of topics that I could talk about.

Secondly, derivatives were being used more in institutional portfolios at that time, so having a background in derivatives was helpful in considering whether to hedge exposure or not. The idea of synthetic exposure was starting to become more and more in favor. That was a differentiator for me in my career at the University of Wisconsin as we started to think about those things, rather than just hiring managers. That helped me during the interview for my position. We did a few things that were helpful for the portfolio; for instance, we hedged a certain exposure perfectly before 2008.

Overall, my interest is a combination of economics and mathematics, which has been fulfilled by both derivatives and institutional investing. In hindsight, it was a more natural fit than I could have ever planned, but it makes sense as I trace through how one thing led to the other.

Trusted Insight: How did you go about hedging the portfolio exposure for the University of Wisconsin Foundation in 2008?

David Erickson: Around 2006 and 2007, like a lot of people, we were getting very nervous about the housing market. In terms of returns, we felt we were getting rewarded for risk that was getting toward the eighth or ninth inning, so we started to look at ways of hedging credit risks. Ultimately, we decided to hedge investment grade credit risk. Our thesis was that if there was a collapse, all credit markets would be impaired. Purchasing "insurance" in investment grade credit markets was still cheap in 2007, and we began to move in that direction.

We put a short credit hedge in the endowment, and it worked great. We put it on around mid-2007, which was maybe the best time to do so. We did not carry it all the way through to March 2009, unfortunately, but we still got a pretty good benefit from it. Of course, we had difficult returns in 2008 like everyone else, but hedging on the edges did help us on a relative basis. My background in derivatives helped me start asking questions such as "if we can't do it through a manager, could we do it synthetically? And how would we execute that?"

I also have to give credit to my investment committee at the University of Wisconsin. I had a number of really good investors there who were constantly pushing and asking questions like "If we think things are expensive, why aren't we going to cash?" or "Why aren't we hedging our exposure?" I was always being challenged by that group, and it was a great education for me.

Trusted Insight: There have been some cracks in Q4 2015 and Q1 2016, and some investors are a little hesitant. How would you compare the 2008 market with the current market?

David Erickson: I compare the market today to two different environments. In some ways, 2015 felt like 1999 in that tech stocks have done much better than the rest of the market. We talked a lot at Ascension Investment Management and also with our institutional clients about the idea that if you're a value investor, you really have not been rewarded in the last couple of years, so how long should you hold that conviction? Over time, value investing does matter. There has been some really close similarities to 1999.

There have also been some similarities to 2006 and 2007. We have been asking ourselves, "Where do things look inexpensive that we can overweight? Where is there value?" If there's an area we think is expensive, we want to rebalance. It's a struggle to find where we want to put the money to overweight as an offset to an underweight, because everything seems to be fairly priced or on the expensive side. That is creating some challenges. For us, we are not adding risk beyond where our target risks should be. At the same time, we can't be underweight risk, because there may be a month or two where the Federal Reserve decides to be more aggressive on monetary policy, for instance, and the market rallies really quickly. We've been very neutral across the board trying to pick good managers and deals, and be more specific in our investment choices as opposed to just re-lying on markets.

I think there's a nervousness underlying this. We're getting to the end of how much Central Bank activities can prop up the market, so we ask ourselves every-day what the next environment will look like. Will it rebound and get healthier, or will it bounce around zero for a while? Or could this ultimately crack?

Trusted Insight: In terms of mitigating those market risks by picking good managers and deals, what do you look for?

David Erickson: From the beginning, we set up our recommended asset allocation to be diversified across economic regimes. We were very deliberate in looking for investments that are targeted to do well in growth, inflationary and deflationary environments. We're very tactical in trying to over and underweight firstly across those economic regimes and secondly by what's attractive in terms of asset class within that. Our assets under management are not equally weighted across those economic regimes, as our institutional clients all have different weights. We're trying to stay relatively neutral across our targets until we get more information, because we don't know if the next environment is going to be inflationary or deflationary.

We also spend a lot of time identifying managers who have done relatively well over the past 18 to 24 months. We have more confidence in those who can navi-gate this volatile environment, where returns have been close to zero, as opposed to someone who may have a great 10-year track record. The recent record is more relevant to me right now, because we could see this volatility for a number of years ahead, and I want to have managers that do well in that environment.

Trusted Insight: It has been a challenging year for many hospital systems. How do you think investing within hospital systems is evolving?

David Erickson: I think we all recognize that a hospital system's investments are very important to support the system's continued operation and growth. There-fore, a lot more hospital systems are creating their own investment teams or out-sourcing to those who can help them achieve their objectives. We are also seeing a lot more health care people attending conferences. The health care-only investor groups that I've been a part of contain some of the best investors that I know. They are becoming more sophisticated. These groups are typically very collaborative - very open to sharing reference calls, getting together to talk through markets and conferences are often open books.

At the end of the day, trying to earn a return for the amount of risk each portfolio wants to have is a difficult question no matter what type of portfolio you're invest-ing for, so health care investors are all trying to figure that out.

Trusted Insight: Socially responsible investing (SRI) is still fairly unique within the investment world and has its own special set of challenges. How you approach that aspect of investing?

David Erickson: Our investment guidelines are based on teachings of the Catholic Church. Every Catholic institutional investor's guidelines are a little bit different, but like many Catholic institutional investors, Ascension Investment Manage-ment's SRI guidelines are based on the U.S. Council of Catholic Bishops invest-ment guidelines, but there might be differences in various revenue thresholds.

Tobacco is a good example. Ascension Investment Management will not permit investments in a company that has more than 20 percent of its revenue in tobacco. We have a number of restrictions like that in the way we set up our SRI guidelines. Once we establish those guidelines, we can go through the list of public compa-nies across the world, including emerging market countries. We don't just stop at the United States. We try to establish that list across the globe. We start with a restricted list of over 800 companies. As part of our guidelines, we have a philos-ophy section where we try to capture things that aren't necessarily in black and white. There are a lot of times where we'll come across a situation not captured in the specific guidelines, but it definitely would not be something that we think would promote Catholic teachings. For instance, it might be predatory lending, or it might be environmental, or it might be a social impact on how they're treating their workers.

It's hard to put a rule-based analysis on those companies in a lot of those cases. If there's a question about a name in our portfolio, we work with a Catholic ethicist to determine if we think that's a company that should be sold or if it can stay in the portfolio.

Every quarter, there seems to be an issue where it's not black and white. It's something we want to have a discussion about. We make sure that we discuss these issues with all of our affected clients and how we resolved it. Considerable effort goes into this process. At the end of the day, you have a portfolio that is really avoiding anything we think violates the teachings of the Catholic Church. At Ascension Investment Management, we have our investment people review the portfolio and look at the names. We think the combination of having a restricted list and then applying an overarching philosophy can help us cover those grey areas and takes us as close as we can be.

While the SRI guidelines negatively screen things out, we also like to be proactive in supporting the teachings of the Catholic Church. One way to do that is through "impact investing," which is a phrase that seems to be pretty popular right now. We are trying to identify other investments that not only have a good financial return, but also promote a social good. We identify that as a company or project that either supports the world's poor and vulnerable or promotes good stewardship of our environment. Those two categories cover lots of things. The environment might be clean energy or clean water. The poor and vulnerable might be food, education, health care, etc.

Through that combination of restricting investment in things that violate the teachings of the Catholic Church and investing in things that promote the teachings of the Catholic Church, we think that we are using our money as best as we can. That's not just by doing the underlying mission the clients often have, but within the dollars themselves -- we can be proud of how they're invested and that they can be doing good at the same time.

Trusted Insight: What advice would you would give to someone who is looking to build a career in institutional investing?

David Erickson: Be well read. I'm reading a book right now called *Antifragile: Things That Gain From Disorder* by Nassim Nicholas Taleb. The book talks about how if you're a fragile person or industry as you go through volatility, it makes you weaker. If you're an antifragile person or industry and you go through volatility, it makes you stronger. I think that on the investment side, you have to be ready to go through up periods and down periods. You're never always going to be right. If you're able to develop a team, a psyche and a process, then having that mindset with your group as you go through volatility doesn't shake your conviction, it actually makes you stronger. I think that's really important. In hindsight, 2008 and 2009 were really rough periods to go through, and I think the lessons I learned then made me a better investor. So I would recommend reading that book and then discussing it with someone who has gone through volatility on the job to get an understanding of that. You're going to go through volatility in your career, and managing that while also making yourself stronger is important.

Will New Investment Vehicles Create More Problems Than They Solve?

Dhvani Shah, Chief Investment Officer, Illinois Municipal Retirement Fund

Dhvani Shah is the chief investment officer of Illinois Municipal Retirement Fund, a pension fund with $34.9 billion assets under management. Previously, Shah was the managing director of private equity of the $89.9 billion New York State Teachers' Retirement System. Shah has a BBA from Loyola University and an MBA from the University of Chicago Booth School of Business.

The pension fund currently allocates about $5 billion of capital in private markets and works with 40 external managers investing these assets, the majority of which are small and opportunistic funds. In this interview, Shah discusses IMRF's approach in selecting these funds and the pension fund's strategy to stand out in increasingly saturated private markets.

Shah was named on Trusted Insight's 2017 Top 30 Women Chief Investment Officers. She graciously spoke with us on February 27, 2017.

Trusted Insight: Recently, several notable women chief investment officers across endowments, pension funds and family offices have resigned or retired. What does it mean to you to be one of the women thought leaders of the industry?

Dhvani Shah: To be a thought leader in the industry, to me, means being a good role model and mentoring talented individuals who are interested in their professional growth. That means developing tomorrow's leaders. I value sound judgment, ability to think critically and proactively. I believe in continuous learning and value intellectual curiosity. As a leader in the industry, it's important to demonstrate these traits as well as support the development of these traits in your staff.

Trusted Insight: When looking to hire a new staff member, how do you go about approaching the idea of diversity?

Dhvani Shah: Whenever I am speaking at various conferences, and specifically, I speak at many that are focused on diversity, I put the word out on IMRF. When I have a position opening, I am able to attract talented staff. Once you attract talented staff, you need to have structure in place to retain and develop that talent. We support, for example, the CFA and CAIA programs, which facilitate professional development.

Trusted Insight: How does the IMRF strategy avoid a herd mentality in increasingly saturated private markets?

Dhvani Shah: We are differentiated based on our team approach and portfolio construction. For example, our private market program is monitored by a team of four professionals and includes real estate, private equity, agriculture and timber investments.
Monitoring this $5+ billion portfolio across about 40 firms gives this team breadth and depth when it comes to understanding the private market landscape. That is what allows us to take advantage of the market opportunity across the sub asset classes.

The second differentiator is our portfolio construction itself. We are thoughtful about what we add to our portfolio, so that we have time and capital for the investment managers in our portfolio. This approach differentiates us because most institutional private markets portfolios are much larger in terms of number of managers.

Trusted Insight: With that maturation, there is a push into different investment vehicles outside of the typical ten-year lock up, two-and-twenty model. Is that a fundamental shift in private markets away from two-and-twenty and toward a more tailored approach? Or are these just more tools in the toolbox?

Dhvani Shah: The institutional investor space has many different investment models. For the larger investors, this new trend in vehicles outside of the ten-year lock up and two-and-twenty model is another tool in the toolbox.

I do believe that the longer lock up periods and the carried interest model may pose an alignment of interest issue. From my perspective, the jury is out whether the new vehicles solve more problems than they create.

Trusted Insight: What potential problems might they create?

Dhvani Shah: In your typical private equity fund, with a European waterfall, you actually have a set of mechanisms for the carried interest calculations.

But when it's a longer time period, such as a permanent vehicle, how is the carried interest calculated on an open-ended fund? Is it still based on divestments or on valuations over a time period? If it is the latter, the investor is still invested in the asset while the General Partner is getting carried interest.

Whether this alignment of interest is strong or not, really depends on the details of those vehicles. That is why I said that the jury is out because you really have to evaluate each of those strategies based on the mechanics with which some of these economics are being calculated.

Trusted Insight: You have 40 managers on the private side. To what degree are you shifting away from some of those more monolithic, giant managers toward either a new manager or a niche strategy?

Dhvani Shah: To put our portfolio into perspective, we do have two evergreen separate accounts, where it's a manager program and then the remaining investments are made directly by staff, which is the portfolio of about 40 managers. Our evergreen separate account portfolios give us this broad exposure, and then what we do directly needs to be more opportunistic.

In our direct funds portfolio, we have venture capital, buyout, growth, credit and special situations. And yes, to date, we actually do not have any direct investments in the mega buyout funds.

Trusted Insight: What's the rationale behind avoiding the larger funds with notable names? Is it a function of your AUM and average check size? Is it the fund's being late in its lifecycle? Is it something else?

Dhvani Shah: We found that we already had exposure to the larger funds through our evergreen separate accounts, and we decided to focus on the smaller and opportunistic funds.

Our strategy is also related to the check size that we write versus the size of the mega funds. We would prefer to have an advisory board seat. We would like to have a voice at the table. So the size of our equity might not be large enough to get that seat at the table, which would prevent us from investing in those mega buyout funds.

Trusted Insight: You've been at Illinois Municipal for a little more than five years now. How has your mindset, your approach toward the portfolio and markets evolved over that time?

Dhvani Shah: There are two major areas of difference. First is that we now have a direct funds portfolio. Before I joined, there were no direct private equity fund investments. Second is the change in market landscape. There's always something new, whether it's new strategies or new vehicles. Five years ago, you would not have thought about some of these permanent fund vehicles in a private market.
From the market landscape, some of the terms have changed to be more focused on transparency in the past few years. The market is definitely adapting to what it takes to stay relevant. The private markets landscape has become more mainstream.

I am even seeing more analytical tools than a couple decades ago. We were always doing our own cash flow modeling and attribution analysis, but now there are definitely more tools for due diligence as well as monitoring.

Trusted Insight: When there's rapid evolution of a market like you described, both long-term trends and fads will develop. How are you differentiating between them?

Dhvani Shah: I determine whether something is a fad or a long-term trend by evaluating the merits of the strategy and seeing if it stacks up to the fundamentals of investing but, only time will tell. Having investment conviction is important to be able to differentiate fad from trend.

Trusted Insight: The number and sophistication of capital allocators continues to grow. What challenges does that present to you or more broadly to chief investment officers within the industry?

Dhvani Shah: In this space, there's always this question: is there too much capital chasing too few good deals? I think that's always been part of the evaluation of the strategy. I don't know if that is a new risk.

I do think that the one thing that has changed over the past couple of decades is alignment of interest between Limited Partners (LP). Normally, you think about GP-LP alignment. Now with different models and different investors, there are preferences of capital is deployed -- whether it's a commingled fund, co-investments, direct JVs with the manager, permanent vehicles. Now there are issues that you have to think about within LPs. Is an LPAC member voting in a certain manner because their firm owns a portion of the manager or has heavy co-invest deal flow from that manager?

Trusted Insight: How does Illinois Municipal differ from your peers?

Dhvani Shah: Our assumed rate of return is 7.5 percent. We beat that return on a five-year basis ending December 31, 2016, with our gross return of 9.52 percent and net return of 9.28 percent, versus a benchmark of 8.82 percent, based on preliminary data.

Why is that important? It allows us to invest per our strategic plan, and as a long-term investor in the private markets asset class. You can be the attractive source of capital for those top-tier managers. Having strong organizational governance and funding stability has allowed us to deploy capital in the private market methodically. And we do become a premier LP that a manager would want capital from.

Trusted Insight: Private markets are all about access. How important is it to be seen as a premier LP?

Dhvani Shah: In my mind, that's our edge. We do not have a $300 million check to write for each fund. So, if you're not the largest check writer, then you need to be a unique, sound and stable LP.

So, what makes us attractive? The way we formed our private markets team across asset classes also is unique because that means that IMRF team has a different viewpoint.

When I see a vehicle in the private equity side, I've actually seen some of those already on the real estate side. I'm talking mechanically. The open-ended core real estate vehicle sound a little similar to some of the things we were seeing on a private equity site. So, it's kind of interesting how you can pick some things from different asset classes and have a unique perspective.

And so at the end of the day, being a valued LP is attractive and important.

A Nuanced Evolution Toward Asset Allocation
Lawrence Kochard, Chief Investment Officer, University Of Virginia Investment Management Company

Lawrence "Larry" Kochard is the chief investment officer and CEO at the University of Virginia Investment Management Company, which has $8 billion in assets under management. Previously, Kochard served as the chief investment officer at Georgetown University and the managing director of equity and hedge fund investments at the Virginia Retirement System. Kochard holds a B.A. in economics from the College of William & Mary, an MBA from the University of Rochester and a Ph.D. in economics from the University of Virginia.

In this interview, Kochard discusses how UVIMCO sticks to its strengths to avoid a herd mentality, the difficulties of scaling a co-investment program and the evolution of his approach to markets and institutional investment over his tenured career as an asset allocator.

Kochard was named to Trusted Insight's 2017 Top 30 Endowment Chief Investment Officers. He graciously spoke with Trusted Insight on February 24, 2017.

Trusted Insight: The Yale Endowment model is ubiquitous throughout the industry. How do you see that strategy evolving over time?

Larry Kochard: It's a good question. First of all, most people think the endowment model is as simple as just having a lot of illiquid alternatives, but I would view it a little more nuanced than that. We, more than most asset owners, have an ability to think and act like long-term investors. So many investors have become increasingly short term, and as a part of that means you can handle more liquidity risk. I would agree with that, but I don't think it's as simple as saying we have a high degree of illiquid alternatives. It's more like we have this edge in being a long-term investor. Between the needs of the institution and the way most institutions are governed, that's attractive.

In terms of how that results in a lot to private investments, the challenge is as more money is allocated to private strategies, the prices that are paid by some of those private managers are going up, and we're later in the economic cycle. Now this becomes tough.

There's now a better appreciation on the part of most investors that we're in a lower return world. Fees take a disproportionately larger part of the gross return. Private investments have continued to go up in terms of commitments. Managing that is difficult.

What does it mean for us? Where you saw many large endowments looking relatively similar over time, there might be more of a parting of people that have slightly different asset allocation strategies.

Trusted Insight: There is a finite amount of investments being pursued by near-infinite capital, which creates a herd mentality. How do you go about differentiating UVIMCO?

Larry Kochard: I'm a firm believer in playing to our strengths. Some of our allocation may be the result of some views that we have in terms of where there might be a lack of capital, and where there's relatively attractive pricing, which is getting harder and harder to find.

A big chunk of where we are, in terms of how we allocate, is playing to our strength. Across every strategy, there is a distribution of median performance for managers to bottom quartile to top quartile, to possibly top decile. We will have a greater or lesser allocation to something to the extent that there are certain strategies in which we have more of an advantage to understand that space, get access to the top managers, be able to identify upcoming managers early in their life cycle. Some of our allocation is influenced by that capability, which could change over time.

You don't want to say "Over the last year, or last five years, the top performing endowment had allocation of 10% or 20% to X and we only had 5%. Let's boost ours just because others were successful." That's kind of exact opposite of the way it works here.

We are looking to find those areas where there are managers that have the ability to deploy capital in attractive prices and have an ability to make good investments, and we are better suited for identifying who these managers are and getting access to those managers. That strength will wax and wane over time and is influenced by the institution and its alumni.

Getting back to the endowment model, an advantage that endowments have relative to other asset owners is the fact that we have alumni. It really helps us identify interesting opportunities and get access to those opportunities by leveraging that alumni network.

Trusted Insight: With the maturation of private markets, there is a push to various investment structures. Is there a fundamental change in private markets away from the 2-and-20 model?

Larry Kochard: At an extreme, the way to get away from that is to just build that capability in house to do direct investing. It is unlikely we will be able to attract and keep people who are as good as those who work for top private equity firms. If they're that good, they probably would go out on their own and charge 2 and 20.

There have been other asset owners that have been more successful doing direct investing. Some of the large Canadian pensions have done a good job of building in-house capability on the private side, where they have the ability to write big checks. Again, getting back to the notion of playing to your strengths.

What we do instead, in order to cut into those fees, is look for opportunities to co-invest, or develop relationships with fundless sponsors. That way you can invest directly, but not within a high-fee fund structure. However, you must assess if there is an adverse selection problem. So, it's about making sure you can get over that hurdle.

We look at co-investments, but it's hard to scale. We do a little more co-investments now than we used to, but it's not as though it'll be a large percentage of what we do. I think if you try to scale it, it would not be additive to returns.

Another way you can try to cut into the fees is to develop relationships with groups early in their life cycle. This way you can be one of their cornerstone investors until they get their footing and carve out attractive fees. Again, I don't want to overemphasize that.

I think there's been a lot of asset owners that have talked about renegotiating fees. The challenge you come up with is that oftentimes those that are most willing to renegotiate are the funds that you may be less likely to want to be invested with. I don't want to overstate that either, but I think you are seeing some movement on that front, very little but some, and then, some co-investing.

Trusted Insight: You've been with UVIMCO for six years. With respect to your long-term perspective, in what nuanced ways has your approach to the portfolio changed over that period?

Larry Kochard: In terms of what's changed, it is pretty nuanced. A) Our total allocation to private investments has been slowly going down. B) I have a greater appreciation for the need to, when something is less liquid, have it be appropriately sized as a smaller part of the portfolio over time. C) There are a number of active managers that we've used historically to add value net of what you could get from a passive exposure. When you really properly account for that, I don't think the alpha may be quite as strong as what people may have believed, historically.

We stick with our managers for a long time. There's a constant replenishing. Sometimes when managers get too big, we replace them with managers that are smaller and earlier in their life cycle. That constantly evolves. I don't think there's any big dramatic change that I've seen.

Trusted Insight: What are the private market allocations being replaced by over time?

Larry Kochard: That's a good question. What has replaced that over time are more concentrated public managers. These are managers that take a friendly approach to activism and take a private equity approach to investing in the public market. Some of those strategies are still relatively high fee and are also relatively illiquid versus a typical public equity manager. They're also relatively low turnover, meaning they're holding their positions for years. They develop close relationships with the company and are able to truly act like a long-term shareholder in a constructive way, as opposed to just being a passive shareholder.

It's about looking at companies and being able to try to add value to companies in a similar way to private managers. Although there's a lot more in the way of activism today than in the past, it's still attractive relative to what has become an increasingly competitive environment for a lot of private strategies.

But again, has that been a big change? No. It's been a very small change.

Trusted Insight: What topics are you and your staff grappling with right now?

Larry Kochard: The thing that everyone grapples with are a lot of the geopolitical risks right now, but I don't they're any bigger now than they've ever been. People always think the current geopolitical risks are higher than ever, but, whether it's what is happening in Europe, or what's happening in China, or what's happening with the politics in the U.S., there are too many people that try to predict some of those outcomes and fail.

One of the things that we try to stay focused on is not getting paralyzed or fixated on our inability to forecast those things; sticking to our knitting of partnering with great managers for long periods of time; and making sure we can find new ones and know when to trim existing ones.

With that said, are there other long-term themes in which we can really make an overweight to and stick with that for a long period of time? And again, it's been harder to find some of those more recently. I think the big thing is to just not become paralyzed with a lot of these macro fears.

Trusted Insight: There's been an increasing number and sophistication of institutional investment offices. Does that present a challenge in differentiating from the herd?

Larry Kochard: The number of additional competitors has been a growing concern. That makes our ability to get access to great funds that much more difficult. Not only has it been an issue, but it will continue to be an issue for us.

That's why we need to, in addition to trying to find those managers, think of some themes that we can capitalize on. What are ways to differentiate ourselves from some of those other investors, as we are long-term partners with some of these great managers? Without a doubt, that creates a challenge for us.

Trusted Insight: I'm in the process of reading your book, where you interview a number of CIOs. If you were to conduct a similar CIO interviews today, what would you ask them?

Larry Kochard: Wow, that's a really good question. I think some of the questions you asked are really good. How have your views changed?

Getting back to that question of how I've changed, I laid out the different asset classes in the first few chapters of the book, whether it was private equity, hedge funds, real estate, etc. The evolution that I've made from then to today, which started at Georgetown and has continued here, is the notion that endowments should not be filling up buckets.

Instead, we have an overall level of market risk, which is influenced by these three broad asset classes, which are public equity, public bonds and public real estate. Equities, bonds and real assets. That sets a certain level of market risk that we want to attain, but then we manage to that level of market risk by finding what we think are the best assets across an array of different levels of risky assets. The riskiest are venture capital, and the lowest risk being cash, in terms of just volatility. That sets a market risk budget.

Then we separately have a liquidity risk budget that is a maximum amount of illiquidity we're able to handle, in terms of unfunded commitments, as well as percentage of our pool that can be turned into cash within a certain period of time.

When we assess whether we should allocate to a real estate manager, a resources manager or a buyout manager, they're all competing for this unfunded commitment capital. This is a certain cost to us.

It leads to a very different way of thinking about investments, as opposed to just saying, we're gonna have a certain target allocation to real estate, a certain target allocation to buy-out, a certain target allocation to venture. We try to allocate and commit to a level that gets us to that target. It allows us to be a little more thoughtful and play some of those opportunities against each other.

Getting back to your prior question, I would actually turn this question to each of the CIOs: How have your thoughts evolved over time, in terms of how you think about what influences the way you allocate to different strategies? That's why I call them strategies and not asset classes.

At an extreme, there've been some institutions that have gone even further than this. Ultimately, the big risk that I have in my portfolio is equity market risk, and I manage to an equity market risk that is equivalent to a beta of about 0.7 to public equities.

At the extreme, the other institutions that take on the smart beta have said, "We're gonna have a target to equity risk, and then a target to these other factor exposures -- say value, or small cap, or quality. Maybe we'll match 'em."

The reason I don't go quite that far is in that all of our investments, for the most part, are in commingled funds with varying degrees of transparency. I don't think I have enough data to truly understand what those factor exposures are. It's hard to estimate with any degree of confidence. I think it gives people a false sense of precision.

Your exposure to equity market sensitivity or risk, since that really drives most movement in returns, is easier to get your arms around. That's why I have this middle ground, versus others that have gone even further of managing to these factor exposures. We just manage to one factor exposure: equity risk.

I would ask some of the CIOs how their thinking has evolved. Are they just trying to fill up buckets? On our team, another thing that's changed is I've moved to more of a generalist approach, where people have their specialty, but people on the team actually have an ability to get involved outside of that specialty. Everything is very team oriented, in terms of the way we approach thinking on any one investment. That way you just don't have the real estate person finding more real estate to fill up a real estate bucket.

I would ask the other CIOs: has their thinking evolved on that front, both in terms of the way they think about those asset classes, as well as the way they've organized their teams to manage on a day-to-day business?

I think there are more people that use that now than if you go back ten years, when we wrote the book. You can tell by writing the book, that it wasn't the way I was operating. It was shortly after writing the book that my thinking on the matter actually evolved.

This Policy-Driven Market 'Really Scares Me'

Mark Canavan, Senior Portfolio Manager, New Mexico Educational Retirement Board

Mark Canavan is senior portfolio manager at the New Mexico Educational Retirement Board where he manages the pension funds' $1.7 billion in real estate and real assets allocations. During his time at the Retirement Board, Canavan has expanded the scope and definition of what it means to invest in the real assets space to achieve stellar returns, all while battling through some of the toughest market conditions in recent history and a near fatal bout with cancer.

Canavan was named on Trusted Insight's 2016 Top 30 LPs Investing In Real Estate & Real Assets, and he graciously spoke with us on November 4, 2016.

Our conversation was broken into three parts: first, Canavan's implementation of mitigation banking to revitalize distressed areas of nature and generate a double-digit IRR; second, Canavan's first-hand account of stumbling onto the impending financial calamity known as the Great Recession and derisking the New Mexico Treasury's portfolio (his previous employer) before the collapse; and finally, Canavan's outlook on the current market climate and its implications on real estate and real assets.

The following piece is part three of the interview. With those experiences (and his broader career) in hindsight, we asked Canavan about the current state of the markets and how he has positioned the real assets portfolio to mitigate risk while generating the best-possible returns over the near and long term.

Trusted Insight: What do you make of the current market situation?

Mark Canavan: It really scares me.

Over a year ago at a conference, I brought up the fact that at the Treasurer's Office, if I wanted to sell everything, it was a few keystrokes. You're out. Now, at ERB, we're in these long-term vehicles.

The panel moderator asked, "What are you going to do?"

I said in front of the whole room, "If I could, I'd sell, but I'm long all this stuff. This is not easy to get out of." I'm very conflicted about that. I've talked to my CIO about building a cash position. I haven't done it yet.

I'm concerned that this is a policy market. It is not driven by economics. This market is driven by policy, specifically interest rate policy, monetary policy. That's what's keeping the market up.

You saw it last summer when the Fed said, "We're going to increase rates." Markets started tanking overnight based on that news. So the Fed said, "Okay, maybe not now." And, the market recovered a little bit.

My call at the Treasurer's Office was based on boatloads of anecdotal experience, and my looking at a situation going, "Wow, this looks just like back then, except worse." Right now, I don't have any anecdotal roadmap to tell me what goes from here, and it scares me.

I know for sure we will be deleveraging our economy and the world's economy for a mind-numbingly long period of time. Early in the financial crisis I was telling people, "We're Japan, man. We'll be trying to re-inflate ourselves out of this for decades." That, to me, is the best case scenario. I'm really worried about deflation.

Bridgewater's research would say, "This is a beautiful deleveraging. It will happen over time, and they've got the right balance of government spending and pumping money into the economy." And, I hope they're right.

The problem with what they've done with the economy: how they structured the bailout and how they structured saving the economy, in my opinion, was totally wrong. What they've done is stratified socio-economic classes. We're locked in.

Social mobility between classes now just went way down, and the middle class is going to continue getting pinched.

Because they've stratified the economy, the rate of return on normal publicly traded investments is going to be low. Stock markets are not going to provide the performance they did during the 80s or 90s. It's not going to have the historical eight or nine percent rate of return. Bonds aren't going to deliver for sure, and even the private equity markets have gotten pretty compressed.

Trusted Insight: You've discussed how mitigation banking has worked out for your portfolio. Besides that, how does your market outlook translate into investment strategy? How do you approach your portfolio when you must take both an inherently long-term perspective, but also meet annual payout requirements?

Mark Canavan: I'm glad you brought that up, and I hate you for bringing that up too, because it's really prescient.

Real Estate

What that means for my investment decisions right now is I backed off of core real estate. It's been my mantra. I don't want to do core real estate, because cap rates just got so low.

Should I be wrong about deflation and should there be inflation, you don't want to be in low-interest rate, long duration, compressed risk premia real estate when interest rates start going back up. That's a really bad day.

We've done a lot of value add. We're building and selling to core players, and we're still heavy in distressed debt. Gosh, at one point, I can't remember what percentage of my portfolio was distressed debt, but we were heavily overweight. I think we had 40 percent distressed debt at one point.

This is why my real estate fund really just knocks the cover off all of our benchmarks. A few good decisions can make for a good decade.

Cash

In real estate, we're just trying to be as defensive as we possibly can within the kind of structure we have. I warmed up my CIO to the idea of selling out of some profitable positions to just build cash. We purposefully have an allocation to REITs for just such purposes. So we can be more flexible moving in or out of the market. When we do reduce exposure, it will be by selling down our REIT exposure.

At the Treasurer's office, all we really did was not continue to buy, right? I hate to make light of what I did. It's not like I shorted the market and went, "Whoa, I really know what's going on." I knew what was going on, but it's not like I had to make a judgement call on longer term assets – particularly limited partnership structured funds where you are going to take a haircut. But, at ERB it's a different proposition. I want to be defensive here. I want to build cash. I don't want to do core for sure.

Agriculture

I'm spending more time on agriculture now. Prices have sold off recently, yet demographics favor it over the long term. If we do have inflation, agriculture will act as an inflation hedge, and if we go deflationary, it's defensive. After all, people always have to eat.

A colleague told me this little factoid: on a relative basis during the Depression, the one thing that actually didn't go down was almond paste. It was used in a host of baked goods, candies and flavoring – everything from penny candies to high-end cakes. Bottom line is food is highly defensive. Obviously, you still have to buy at the right price. And, it is important to have low-to-no leverage.

Whether you go deflationary or hyper inflationary, there are a lot of things you don't need to buy. I don't have to buy another DVD, or download. I don't have to buy another gig on the cloud. There's all kinds of things I don't have to have, but I still have to eat.

Infrastructure

Infrastructure, same thing. We stopped doing core infrastructure a long time ago. We want to build stuff and sell it to the mega funds. If there's anything I know about the securities world: when there's a huge pile of cash needing to be invested and a bunch of sheep running into a market, which is the situation in infrastructure right now, you want to sell into that. You don't want to be one of those sheep.

There's these huge monolithic funds chasing infrastructure assets that are already overvalued, at very low interest rates and in a historically low interest rate environment. I'd rather sell into that crowd.

I was on a panel with a guy from a huge fund manager. He goes, "Well, Mark, I hate to argue with you, but we have $12 billion of capital invested with us that says your opinion is wrong." And I said, "That's the crowd I want to sell to." It was kind of funny.

That's the strategy we're doing here. We're not necessarily always building something to sell to core, but we're not doing flat out core. Well, that's not true. We recently just did a flat out core infrastructure deal, but it's got a 10 percent coupon. It's a regulated utility in New Zealand, high stability, good regulatory environment and a great coupon. I'll take that all day long.

Water

Lastly, while we may be looking for ways to reduce our real estate exposure, we are seeking ways to increase exposure to water-related investments – water rich farmland or ranchland, water rights, water efficiency, water filtration, water transfers, fallowing programs, water quality programs. Our mitigation banking program touches on water quality and watershed natural filtration ecosystems. Then our infrastructure program gives us exposure to water utilities and desalination. Lastly, we have a water rich property investment that incorporates several themes – water transfers, water efficiency, conservation strategies and fallowing. Still though, we are looking for ways to increase our exposure to water.

The Art Of Doing Nothing
Steve Edmundson, Investment Officer, Nevada PERS

Steve Edmundson is the investment officer at the Public Employees' Retirement System of Nevada (NVPERS). As a one-man team, he oversees all aspects of the system's $34.9 billion (as of 2016) investment program, including investment operations, compliance, research, manager oversight and implementation of investment strategy.

Nevada's pension fund is known for its simple and conservative portfolio strategy despite an increasing trend of complex investment strategies pursued by many of its pension peers. In this interview, Edmundson explains why his simple model is just as good as any other investment model and why doing nothing is something.

Edmundson was named on Trusted Insight's 2016 Top 30 Public Pension Chief Investment Officers. He spoke with Trusted Insight on November 15, 2016.

Trusted Insight: Tell me about the investment office and governing body.

Steve Edmundson: We have one of the more unique investment teams in the industry. I'm the only investment employee here in Nevada.

Our board is comprised of seven public employees, either actively working or retired. The investment staff makes recommendations and the board either approves or doesn't approve those recommendations.

Trusted Insight: What is your investment strategy within private markets, and how has it evolved over time?

Steve Edmundson: The private market strategy has been fairly consistent being targeted at 10 percent of total fund assets. I think the last time it was changed was

2009. It's a fairly conservative structure. Our private real estate allocation entirely consists of unlevered, fully-leased core assets, which is also consistent with our total fund structure. We have a focus on high-quality assets throughout the fund, including our private markets allocation. The Nevada model has really become synonymous with simplicity with a focus on keeping costs low and an emphasis on high-quality assets. That kind of high-quality bias is consistent throughout the fund, not just in our private market's allocation.

Trusted Insight: Is there a reason why you favor real estate and private equity over other types of alternative asset classes such as hedge funds?

Steve Edmundson: Yes. We have made an overt decision not to invest in hedge funds, so we have never had a hedge fund allocation. Again, the high-quality focus. But beyond that, we see hedge funds more as a management style rather than a specific asset class, and have never been comfortable with the complexity, lack of transparency and fee structure associated with hedge funds. They just haven't found a spot. Hedge funds aren't consistent with our overall high-quality, simple approach to investing.

Trusted Insight: What's your view on applying the endowment model to public pensions?

Steve Edmundson: We're kind of the opposite of the endowment model, and we've had a lot of success with that. However, that doesn't mean that I think that the endowment model can't work well. It is more of a question of what fits the comfort level and culture of each particular fund. I think that the endowment model can be a successful approach, and a number of funds have certainly proven that they can be successful with that approach. However, what works for one fund won't necessarily work for another. In our case, I don't think that the endowment approach would be successful in Nevada.

At the same time, however, because we've had success with a simple approach doesn't mean it would necessarily fit the culture of another fund, and may fail, because in order for any strategy to succeed, the people who invest in it need to stick with it when it becomes difficult. If you can't stick with it, then it's going to be a failure, and so the question becomes -- Are you able to stick with it? Does this fit what your constituents want you to be invested in? Does it fit with the culture of your state? Does it fit with the culture of your fund in general? If it does and you're able to apply it across all time periods, then I think ultimately it can be successful.

I think that the endowment model is not going to go anywhere in terms of being utilized, and at the end of the day it probably has as good of a chance of succeeding as any other model as long as it's applied consistently across all market cycles. You have to stick with it.

Trusted Insight: How do you manage to not be swayed by temporary market ups and downs, popular opinions, etc. and stick to your strategy?

Steve Edmundson: We have been doing it this way for so long that discipline and patience are built into our fund's DNA. In fact, if we started acting on current sentiment or short-term market moves, I think it would raise some eyebrows. We know who we are as investors and so do our constituents.

Trusted Insight: Many pensions that invest in alternative assets are terminating such terms, such as hedge funds. Do you think they're overreacting?

Steve Edmundson: While I can't speak to what other funds are doing specifically, I do think that's partially in response to the fee structure, and obviously that performance in the hedge fund industry has suffered over recent years. The combination of those two things are really why that's happening.

Whether or not hedge funds would be a fit in somebody else's portfolio is a tough thing for us to make a call on, because other funds are structured differently and they may very well be comfortable with the complexity and the fees associated with hedge funds if they think that provides them with the return streams that they're looking for.

Trusted Insight: In the history of the NVPERS, were there any market turbulences that put this simple structure in significant risks?

Steve Edmundson: There's certainly been volatile markets where our returns have reacted accordingly and our assets' growth has acted accordingly. However, I'd say that any long-term investor that has significant exposure to risk assets whether they're stocks, private equity, real estate or high-yield bonds, should expect some volatility. We certainly are not immune to the ups and the downs of markets – 2008 and 2009 come to mind – but we did well on a relative basis, because our high-quality bias served the fund well over that time.

I think that as much as anything else, as long-term investors we should expect those time periods. They're going to happen, they have happened, and they will happen again. What's part of being a disciplined, long-term investor, is looking past those time periods and not changing strategy when they inevitably happen.

Trusted Insight: In the current low-return environment, do you see a trend in the near term that public pensions are moving capital into low-cost, passive investment products?

Steve Edmundson: Lower absolute returns have likely influenced the migration toward indexing. If returns are lower, fees consume a greater portion of an investor's return. So yes, I think that is part of the reason. However, ultimately, I think the bigger reason indexing is gaining in popularity is simply because it is the most efficient way for investors to get the specific market exposures they want in their portfolios.

Trusted Insight: What do you like most about working at a public pension?

Steve Edmundson: I think that the most exciting thing about working for a public pension is that, unlike a lot of jobs, I never forget why I'm here. Our job is to ensure that the investment portfolio does its job for our members and beneficiaries. Every day I see myself coming to work for the 150,000 members who are public employees of our system. I feel pretty good about that. I feel good about getting to do something that I feel is worthwhile and can positively influence the hard-working public employees of the State of Nevada. I believe in what we're doing and that is the most exciting thing about working for Nevada PERS.

More so than the investments. I enjoy the investment stuff very much as well, and obviously that's why I'm here, but doing it for something that you believe in is what makes it worthwhile.

Trusted Insight: What career advice would you give to young people who look to enter public pensions or institutional investing overall?

Steve Edmundson: I would say patience. Be willing to put in the time and always remember what the organization is there to do from the get-go, whether it's an endowment or a public pension. As a pension, we're here to support public employees. So, be patient with their chosen career path and always keep in mind why they've decided to go down the path of being a public employee. I think it's always important to remember that.

And on the investment side, I would advise younger people in the industry not to lose sight of the big picture. Investment decisions should always relate back to the impact on the total fund. It becomes easy to spend too much time and place too much importance on things that don't move the needle.

The Secret Of Making An Endowment Model Successful
Stuart Mason, Chief Investment Officer, University of Minnesota Foundation

Stuart Mason is the associate vice president and chief investment officer of the University of Minnesota Foundation, which has $2.2 billion of assets under management, as of December 31, 2016. Mason is also the portfolio manager for the endowment's venture capital allocation.

Previously, Mason spent 15 years as a senior investment banker and executive officer in several investment banks including Dougherty & Company, EVEREN Securities and Dain Rauscher Corporation. He also served for 10 years as a vice president of Wells Fargo Corporation. Mason holds an MBA from the University of Minnesota and a B.A. in chemistry and biology from St. Olaf College.

Mason was named on Trusted Insight's 2016 Top 30 Endowment Chief Investment Officers. He graciously spoke with Trusted Insight on March 8, 2016.

Trusted Insight: Your portfolio, and that of many other endowments, to some degree follow the "Yale model" that David Swenson is often praised for. Does that ubiquity create a herd mentality?

Stuart Mason: At a very high level, the Yale model says "use private investment vehicles to gain more portfolio diversification," and capture the benefit from the illiquidity premium to produce higher long-term returns. To that extent, the devil is in the details. The details that matter are how large is the allocation to private markets that makes sense for your specific portfolio and what kind of private investments are you able to professionally execute.

For smaller endowments, generally speaking, those with a few hundred million dollars, it's not working very well. Part of the reason is that their allocations to private alternatives are relatively modest, and investment offices of those under $1 billion often don't have the depth in their staff to invest directly with managers, or often don't have the ability to gain access to the very best managers. So they resort to using fund-of-funds that are top heavy on fees. No surprise, the results are often disappointing. If one invests 10 percent or 15 percent in a fund-of-funds, it's difficult to see how that becomes a successful strategy.

If an endowment is large enough to support a professional staff with depth and expertise, which typically manage over $1 billion, the game changes. At the University, our strategy has been to have nearly 50 percent in private fund structures, do it all direct and really underwrite very aggressively a variety of private investments where the expectation is high for added value.

Given our size, we can make commitments to smaller funds in almost any asset class. Often our $10 million commitment, for example, to a private fund is meaningful to the fund manager, and if they actually do well, it can be meaningful to us. It "moves the needle."

There are a lot of researches that suggest smaller funds do better than larger funds in virtually every asset class. That's one reason we seek out funds that are $100 million or $250 million, and we generally avoid funds that are $2 billion or $10 billion. We don't do those because it's virtually impossible in our mind to get a three-times-your-money back on a $10 billion fund, like some of the mega private equity funds.

If you're a venture fund raising $100 million and you execute the strategy with success, then it only takes one investment to return the fund or return a multiple of the fund. While our strategy differs somewhat for each asset class, across the board, you could say that we seek niche opportunities that are often addressed by smaller fund managers. When we do the underwriting of each of these, we are underwriting with an expectation of some return that is significantly higher than just the mean for that asset class.

Trusted Insight: What do you look for in a manager?

Stuart Mason: I've described at least a portion of our strategy as small and niche, which in our minds does not always translate to new managers. While we have done some first-time funds that have GPs that we have known for some time and have confidence in or have invested previously with, we would much prefer to invest in a fund that is sized appropriately for the opportunity and with a manager that has a history and has sponsored funds before.

We basically look for the same thing in every private fund manager: a meaningful enough history of consistently addressing an asset class that we have determined is an attractive market. In venture, for example, a vast majority of our investments are with managers who are addressing big data analytics, enterprise moving to mobile platforms, consumer marketplace solutions, SaaS services and AI or machine learning. If it isn't in these sectors, we probably aren't interested. That narrows the field.

With those criteria, we've narrowed the field to a relatively modest number of fund managers who are 30 or 40 something years old and have been doing this long enough to have developed a reference network in an industry segment and an investment record that indicates success. We have selected these industry segments, and we prioritize the kind of manager or teams that we want to invest in because we think there is a persistent long-term opportunity to big data analytics and AI, etc. This isn't a new idea, but there's a lot of innovation in this technology sector. If you can pick a couple of funds that do that well, they may have a tailwind for a decade.

We don't feel the same comfort level with our understanding of biotech, so we don't do much biotech, even though some investors have done quite well. For another example, we don't think consumer products -- dating websites, games, grocery shopping and things like that -- are persistent trends with clear market differentiators. Some of them are going to turn out to be just great, but hundreds of them are likely to do poorly. So we're not interested in those market segments.

We go through a thematic approach to narrow the scope for each of the asset classes. So our approach is the same for value added or opportunistic real estate, commodities investments and distressed credit investments.

In private equity, for example, we don't do mega-fund private equity where financial engineering plays a big role in return generation. We have in the past, however, learned that higher levels of leverage can work against you in periods of stressed market conditions. So we've refined our strategy in private equity so that we are presently looking at lower mid-market, with certain market cap limits and certain technology or service-related industry segments. It has made it easier to recognize a manager that fits those criteria when we see it.

Our normal due diligence process is fairly straightforward. We try to look at every deal a manager has done. We talk to many of the CEO's of deals that have gone well and those that have done poorly. We try to figure out why some deals worked and others didn't. That's where having a professional staff who really know how to dig deeply, is critical in making any private investment. Funds that are much smaller, say $400 or $500 million dollars, with a staff of only one or two individuals, generally can't hope to make private investments other than through a fund-of-funds vehicle.

Trusted Insight: The past decade has been a time of unprecedented government intervention in the global economy -- quantitative easing, ultra-low interest rates, negative interest rates. How do you strategize in an environment that is frankly unpredictable?

Stuart Mason: I think the quantitative easing (QE) in whatever form it has taken in various developed economies around the globe has inflated asset prices, generally speaking. Stocks, real estate and lots of different examples you could point to where zero interest rates make those assets more expensive. We have, in general, tried to reduce our exposure to those assets that appear to have inflated value because of cheap money strategies around the globe for the past decade.

We have no traditional fixed income for example -- no Barclays Aggregate portfolio, in part because credit spreads are so tight and yield versus the credit risk is low. The fixed income that we do have is in what we refer to as "return-generating fixed income." It is idiosyncratic, niche-y and often takes advantage of themes such as "going where the banks no longer go." All this regulation you referred to means the capital requirements for banks no longer allow them to do this certain kind of subprime lending or certain types of non-investment grade corporate lending. That creates opportunities to create higher yielding portfolios with a managed risk profile. Banks have also largely exited the real estate lending business, which creates other opportunities.

Capital provided to some of these niches has completely evaporated or gone to shadow banking systems in some fashion. Our fixed income book, in total, is half or two-thirds in go-where-banks-don't-go strategies that we underwrite to low mid-teens return targets. This higher yielding portfolio is offset by a smaller slice of TIPS and short-term U.S. Treasuries. This reflects our view that the whole middle section of the fixed income markets is not a productive place to be. As I mentioned, that segment of the market is bearing risks and not getting paid for it.

Trusted Insight: What sets the University of Minnesota Investment Office apart from your peers?

Stuart Mason: First of all, we view our peers as other major educational institutions and some foundations with portfolios anywhere from $1 billion to $5 or $6 billion dollars with a long-term investment horizon.

What distinguishes us from them is that because we are on the smaller end of that spectrum, we can take advantage of smaller, niche managers. An institution that is $5 billion or $10 billion can't write a check or make a commitment for $5 million to a $50 million private equity or venture fund, for example. That size investment just doesn't merit their time and effort for the contribution it might make. While that's not our bread and butter, we have a several of those where we committed $5 or $10 million to smaller funds and, as we have discussed, where our expectation is for potential outsized returns.

Secondly, I think we have exceptional skill in private investment capabilities amongst the six of us on staff here. While we may not have the largest staff, a lot of our peers have fewer people dedicated to the private book, and they struggle to manage a portfolio that's any more than 20 percent or 30 percent private, whereas we are nearly 50 percent. Four or five of us spend most of our time dedicated to the private investments, and we leave the publicly-traded equity portion of the book largely to low maintenance index funds. We just don't have time or bandwidth to try to pick public stock managers, where if we succeed, we earn an extra 50-100 basis points. If we want to underwrite a private equity fund, we may get an extra 500 basis points or 1,000 basis points. I think a focused, exceptional staff working really hard most of the time on private investments is a somewhat different model.

Thirdly, an important factor to success is a governance structure that has a very skilled, committed and engaged investment committee. There are eight members on our investment committee. We meet formally on a quarterly basis. We often also have telephonic meetings in between quarters. All members are professional investors themselves in their day jobs, and they all are really committed to helping us build and manage a pretty complex portfolio. I think their engagement and commitment really extends our ability to make good asset allocation decisions and keeps the bar high on our underwriting strategies.

Trusted Insight: What is the key to success for an endowment CIO?

Stuart Mason: It is my view that we all operate in very dynamic capital markets. They are constantly changing. They're fluid. The opportunity to really add incremental value changes regularly. One of the most important factors is managing risk. It is critical to understand what kinds of risk are imbedded in every investment we make and how those risks are correlated across the portfolio. Without that understanding, it's impossible to properly evaluate any new, incremental investment. After that, I think being constantly open to changes and new ideas is critically important. History has produced many examples where early adopters have reaped the greatest benefit. Of course, new ideas or trends need to be properly vetted, but I can think of examples of timber in the 1990s, technology venture in the past decade, re-insurance and many others. Opportunity can often get arbitraged away. If you decide five years from now to invest in re-insurance, you're likely to be too late. Same as if you decide to invest in discounted mortgage bonds in 2009, you made a killing. If you waited until 2013, the opportunity was not so good.

You also have to have a governance structure that gives you flexibility. You have to have the internal skills to be able to evaluate opportunities and to determine if it fits in your portfolio and adds incrementally to meeting the objectives that your endowment has established. Every one of us has a different set of objectives. What works for us may work for one of my peers just down the street.

Trusted Insight: What trends have you identified that are shaping endowment investing?

Stuart Mason: That's a hard question. Diversification is kind of a fundamental trend that over the last couple of decades has created the engine for the complexity that has emerged in the capital markets. Also, repackaging institutional forms of securities or investment opportunities into institutional quality investment opportunities has been a trend.

When Harvard first invested in timber in the late 90s, they had an early advantage because they identified an attractive asset class, and they could invest directly. By the mid-2000s, there were timber funds that were of institutional quality that gave everybody a chance. I think the packaging of various investment opportunities into institutional quality vehicles gives us all a chance to invest in something new or different, where there might be opportunity. That's clearly a persistent trend. Think of all of the structured finance vehicles that are examples.

There are specific industry or specific asset class trends, as I was alluding to earlier, that we incorporate as thematic investment strategies: Go where the banks aren't, or in technology venture, or perhaps elements of distress credit.

I think unconstrained fixed-income investing has been a trend that all of us have embraced in some form or another over the last few years. It used to be that we all had exposure to the PIMCO or the TCW Total Return Bond Fund. Many endowments have broadened their fixed income strategies and moved away from the Barclays Aggregate benchmark to something much more customized.

I think the trend has been toward niche, segmented investment strategies within asset classes. We've considered that in virtually every asset class. We've narrowed the focus in what we do in real estate for example. We don't have any core real estate anymore; we invest in segments in the value-add or opportunistic sectors.

When we go into a different country like China, we have a very narrowly pre-scribed set of trends that we think are current opportunities in China. We would try to find managers who are investing in those. For example, there are more consumer service-related venture and private equity opportunities that we would purse in China, mostly in the private markets. There are certain niches in real es-tate in China, or in Asia generally, that we think are currently attractive. In Brazil or India, we'd have a different strategy in those geographies.

Maybe the broader answer to your question is: almost everyone has focused more narrowly on the themes that they can execute on, and have conviction in, that they believe will drive acceptable returns. Another example in our portfolio is that we don't have broad emerging markets exposure. We have more focused strategies in each of the larger regions, more focused strategies in India or Latin America or Southeast Asia, rather than just some mandate for broad emerging markets.

The Advantages (And Burden) Of Sovereign Wealth Fund Investing

Yup Kim, Senior Portfolio Manager, Alaska Permanent Fund Corporation

Yup Kim is a senior portfolio manager of Special Opportunities at the Alaska Permanent Fund Corporation (APFC), a $55 billion sovereign wealth fund. This flexible mandate, which represents 20 percent of the Fund's assets, centers primarily on situations stemming from supply and demand imbalances, capital flight, structural complexities or unique opportunities with asymmetric payoffs. The portfolio covers a wide spectrum including direct deals in venture capital and private equity transactions, GP co-investments and strategic stakes and partnerships with investment management firms.

Most recently, Yup was the vice president and an investment committee member at DB Private Equity, the private equity arm of Deutsche Bank with $12 billion of client assets under management. Before that, He worked at Performance Equity, Silver Point Capital and Citigroup. Yup holds a B.A. in economics from Yale University.

Yup was named on Trusted Insight's 2016 Top 30 Sovereign Wealth Fund Rising Stars. Trusted Insight interviewed him on September 28, 2016. In this interview, you will learn about the structure and dynamic of Alaska Permanent Fund's private markets team, the advantages and disadvantages of operating from Alaska, and the unique ability of sovereign wealth funds, as an industry, to embody their country's values – and potentially be hindered by them.

Trusted Insight: You began your career at Citigroup, moved to a hedge fund at Silver Point and then to private equity at Performance Equity and Deutsche Bank before joining Alaska Permanent Fund. What attracted you initially to finance and the investment world?

163

Yup Kim: My childhood experience in an emerging market nonprofit environment cultivated my keen interest in development economics, which led to my first stint at Citigroup's Hong Kong office working on trade and project financing deals with entities like the Asian Development Bank and the World Bank (IFC). Despite its negative media wrap, I soon realized that in the right hands, finance was a powerful tool to spur growth, increase real wages and enrich the lives of the 99 percent, not only those at the top.

Today, what I find unique and fascinating about investing is that everything you consume on a daily basis – every city you visit, every book you read and every conversation you have – can inform your investment decisions and help you become a better investor. Being an investor requires synthesizing large amounts of information to predict what the world might look like in one, five and 20 years, and it has been as fun as it has been rewarding. You are able to, in a small way, dictate the flow of capital to forge what the future might look like.

Trusted Insight: You have seen the industry from a number of unique angles – banking, hedge funds, private equity and now a sovereign wealth fund. How have those experiences informed your investment philosophy?

Yup Kim: My background across various investment firms has offered me some insight on the relative risk-reward tradeoffs across a wide range of strategies. I began my career in credit, which conditioned me to be fairly risk averse and to constantly ask myself, "What could go wrong?" Later, I realized that investing need not to be all pessimistic and began to back capable management teams leading companies enjoying strong, hockey-stick-like growth and looking to disrupt industry incumbents. While the different experiences allow me to pursue opportunities across the risk spectrum and capital structure, capital preservation remains its most important lesson, and it is critical to every decision I make. The market plunge of 2007-2009 reminds me of stress testing each opportunity against a recession or a prolonged risk-off climate, which is becoming increasingly relevant in today's environment.

Trusted Insight: Tell me about the APFC investment team and your role within it.

Yup Kim: The private markets team at APFC includes five team members and covers a broad remit across private equity, special opportunities, infrastructure, private credit and absolute returns. Simply put, our mandate is to add uncorrelated alpha to the broader portfolio. We have an experienced, collegial team with deep backgrounds in both partnership and direct investing, which is essential to what we do. Given our small team, we are required to wear many hats.

Our private equity mandate requires us to be specialists, while the special opportunities mandate requires us to be nimble generalists. In special opportunities, we try to proactively source deals using a themes-driven approach, but not all deals fit into neat labels, which requires flexibility. Overall, intellectual curiosity and the willingness to quickly learn to gain conviction remains critical in this seat and really drives our culture.

Trusted Insight: What challenges do you face as an investor in current market environment?

Yup Kim: Resource constraints remain a challenge, but I am thankful to our leadership and board for thinking long-term and expanding our personnel and organizational capabilities.

Being located far away from the center of deal flows has its obvious disadvantages, but it's worth noting that being away from the buzz and reaffirming soundboards in a hot market helps you form an outsider's perspective and exercise better valuation discipline.

The artificial asset inflation caused by accommodative monetary policies around the globe has trickled down to private assets, and that has certainly been the most challenging part of investing in current market environment.

Trusted Insight: What sectors and geographies are you optimistic about heading into 2017?

Yup Kim: It's been a challenging time to invest. Overall, I think 2016 may be an underperforming vintage year – I'm hoping for some volatility ahead of 2017.

I think most geographies and industries have their share of asymmetric, niche pockets of growth. That being said, in the emerging markets, we're taking a long-term overweight view in India and Brazil, driven both by the demographic growth and consumption basket upgrade story.

While certain technology and life sciences companies command rich valuations in the public markets, we continue to selectively invest in these areas on an earlier stage basis.

Trusted Insight: What characteristics outside of the standard criteria -- repeatable process, proven track record, likeable team -- comprise a good manager or management team?

Yup Kim: Integrity and the spirit of partnership. I think it's increasingly clear who views us strategically and treats us as real partners. I appreciate managers who exhibit humility and emphasize alignment.

Trusted Insight: What medium- to long-term trends are shaping APFC's investment strategy that are unique to sovereign wealth funds?

Yup Kim: There's a deeper appreciation about our ability to leverage the stability and scale of our capital base. Given the absence of a ticking clock to satisfy an annual liability stream, we're able to pursue opportunities which require the resilience to stomach short-term volatility, those which require a longer-term, 10-plus year investment horizon or those that don't fit neatly into an asset class category. As it relates to our scale, we're able to be more assertive and negotiate beneficial terms and better risk-adjusted return matrices through enhanced term sheets or investment structures.

Additionally, while not unique to SWFs, there's a deeper focus and recognition on the importance of building strong investment exposures outside of the U.S. and Western Europe.

Trusted Insight: What sets sovereign wealth funds apart from other institution types?

Yup Kim: Given their source of wealth from natural resources and trade surplus, SWFs typically enjoy a more permanent capital base with the ability to better weather short- to medium-term volatility. SWFs continue to expand in size and importance, and as a result, have had the resources to build an increasingly sophisticated in-house team.

Given their massive scale, SWFs also have the unique ability to export their countries' values through their investments (energy sustainability in Norway, for example), which can dictate what assets and technologies get funded or divested as a reflection of their home country's core set of beliefs.

Finally, certain influential SWFs may encounter increasing hurdles when making investments abroad based on their home country's foreign policy agendas and the ongoing geopolitical climate.

Trusted Insight: What advice would you give to someone aspiring to enter the institutional investing industry?

Yup Kim: Stay curious – be a voracious reader. Investing goes well beyond understanding financial theory and following markets. Equally important is understanding geopolitics, legal and judicial frameworks, economic history, demographic trends, human psychology, biological sciences, disruptive technologies, big picture themes and connecting all the dots.

Stay humble and treat everyone with respect – institutional investing is a people business and emotional intelligence is essential. Be patient, don't overreact to market noise and don't get emotionally tied. Love what you do.

Appendix:

Biographies Of Investors Mentioned In The Book

Aaron Houlihan
Manager of Investments, Catholic Health Initiatives

Aaron Houlihan is the manager of investments at Catholic Health Initiatives. He manages a multi-asset-class portfolio of equity managers, fixed income strategies and private equity investments. Previously, he was a manager of public markets at CenturyLink Investment Management Company and a senior investment analyst of real assets at the University of California. Houlihan has an MBA in finance and entrepreneurship from the University of San Francisco and a B.A. in English from the University of Michigan. He is also a Chartered Financial Analyst and a Chartered Alternative Investment Analyst.

Houlihan was named on Trusted Insight's 2016 Top 30 Hospital Investment Office Rising Stars. He graciously spoke with us on Sep. 29, 2016.

Alan Chang
Partner and Managing Director, Capricorn Investment Group

Alan Chang is a partner and managing director at Capricorn Investment Group. He oversees Capricorn's Asia and emerging markets portfolio and global venture portfolio. Prior to Capricorn, Chang worked at DFJ New England, managing early-stage venture investments, and Montgomery Securities (now Bank of America Securities), advising technology companies on corporate finance. He is an investor in Saildrone, Brilliant.org, Ezetap Mobile Solutions, 21 Inc. and Planet Labs. Chang holds an MBA in general management from Harvard Business School and a B.S. from Duke University, graduating cum laude with a triple major in electrical engineering, computer science and art history. He is also a Chartered Financial Analyst.

Chang was named on Trusted Insight's 2016 Top 30 LP Rising Stars In Venture Capital. He graciously spoke with us on Jan. 13, 2016.

Amy Jensen
Investment Director, Northwest Area Foundation

Amy Jensen is the investment director at Northwest Area Foundation. Previously, she was an portfolio manager at Margaret A. Cargill Philanthropies and an endowment research analyst at Bowdoin College. Jensen holds an MPA in policy analysis and foreign policy from the University of Minnesota --Twin Cities.

Jensen was named on Trusted Insight's Top 30 Foundation Rising Stars. She graciously spoke with us on Mar. 17, 2016.

Ana Marshall
Chief Investment Officer, The William and Flora Hewlett Foundation

Ana Marshall is vice president and chief investment officer for the William and Flora Hewlett Foundation. She is responsible for the asset allocation and strategic investment policy recommendation and implementation of the $9 billion endowment portfolio.

Previously, she served as a senior portfolio manager of global and emerging market equity portfolios at RCM Capital Management. Prior to RCM, Marshall worked as an portfolio manager of emerging market debt and equity portfolios at Bank of America.

Marshall began her career in 1986 as a research analyst of high-yield assets, including corporate debt, distressed debt and emerging market sovereign bonds. Marshall graduated Magna Cum Laude from the University of San Diego in economics and earned her Chartered Financial Analyst designation in 1989.

Marshall was named on Trusted Insight's 2016 Top 30 Foundation Chief Investment Officers and 2017 Top 30 Women Chief Investment Officers. She graciously spoke with us on Oct. 29, 2016 and Mar. 2, 2017.

Andrew Eberhart
Chief Investment Officer, A Family Office

Andrew Eberhart is the chief investment officer at a prestigious single-family office located in Virginia. Previously, Eberhart served as managing director at Lazard Freres & Co., managing partner at the Marshall Fund, managing director at Citigroup Private Bank and U.S. Trust and investment consultant at Cambridge Associates. Eberhart earned a B.A. in economics from Cornell University, actively served for more than a decade as a U.S. Navy aviator and then earned an MBA from University of Pennsylvania.

Eberhart was named on Trusted Insight's 2015 Top 30 Ivy League Graduate Chief Investment Officers. He graciously spoke with us on Nov. 20, 2015.

Anne-Marie Fink
Former Chief Investment Officer, Employee Retirement System of Rhode Island

Anne-Marie Fink was the chief investment officer at the Employee Retirement System of Rhode Island from November 2012 until her departure in June 2016. She oversaw investment of the $7.3 billion defined benefit plan and defined contribution program of the state pension. Prior to joining the pension, she was a managing director at J.P. Morgan Private Bank, managing a portfolio of hedge funds for five years. Fink holds an MBA from Columbia Business School and a B.A. in humanities from Yale University. She has a publication titled "The Money Makers: How Extraordinary Managers Win in a World Turned Upside Down" from the Crown Business in 2009.

Fink was named on Trusted Insight's 2015 Top 30 Ivy League Graduate Chief Investment Officers. She graciously spoke with us on Oct. 29, 2015.

Anthony Breault
Senior Real Estate Investment Officer, Oregon State Treasury

Anthony Breault has been a senior real estate investment officer at the Oregon State Treasury for more than 10 years. Previously, he was a U.S. Navy officer for 22 years. He was also an associate investment manager at Schnitzer West and a general manager at Jones Lang LaSalle. Breault holds a bachelor's degree in international relations from Jacksonville University.

Breault was named Trusted Insight's 2017 Top 30 Public Pension Rising Stars He graciously spoke with us on February 16, 2017.

Asher Noor
Chief Investment Officer and Group CFO, Altouq Group

Asher Noor is a chief investment officer and group chief financial officer at Al-Touq Group, a Saudi Arabian family office. Noor has been based in Saudi Arabia for more than 14 years and is an active public speaker. Prior to Altouq Group, he was the chief financial officer for Morgan Stanley in Saudi Arabia. He also worked for PwC and Banque Saudi Fransi.

Noor has been on the board of many companies in sectors as diverse as aviation, energy, financial services, infrastructure, information technology and telecom, among others, representing AlTouq Group's global investments. He is also the chairman of the leading MENA alternative investments asset manager in UAE. Noor holds an MBA in family business from EDHEC Business School in France and a family business advising certification from the Family Firm Institute in the United States.

Noor was named on Trusted Insight's 2016 Top 30 Family Office Investors. He graciously spoke with us on Nov. 29, 2016.

Baron Koch
Director of Investments, Christus Health

Baron Koch is the director of investments at Christus Health. He oversees the health system's investment function in all aspects. Previously, he was a senior financial analyst of investments within Christus Health. Prior to that, he was a manager of marketing analytics at Torchmark/Liberty National. Koch holds an MBA from The University of Texas at San Antonio and a bachelor's degree in finance from Trinity University. He is also a Chartered Financial Analyst.

Koch was named on Trusted Insight's 2016 Top 30 Hospital Investment Office Rising Stars. He graciously spoke with us on Sep. 28, 2016.

Bartley Parker
Managing Director of Real Estate Investments, Maine Public Employees' Retirement System

Bartley Parker is the managing director of real estate investments at the Maine Public Employees' Retirement System. His responsibilities include developing and presenting new investment ideas for the system's 35 percent commitment to private equity, infrastructure and real assets. Parker joined the pension fund in 2008. Previously, he was a vice president at ICR and a senior research associate at RBC Capital Markets. Parker holds an MBA in general management and finance from Boston University and a bachelor's degree in economics from Westfield State University. He is also a Chartered Financial Analyst and a Chartered Alternative Investment Analyst.

Parker was named on Trusted Insight's Top 30 Future Chief Investment Officers at Pension Funds. He graciously spoke with us on May 5, 2016.

Betty Tse
Chief Investment Officer, Alameda County Employees' Retirement Association

Betty Tse became the first chief investment officer at Alameda County Employees Retirement Association in 2002. Prior to this position, she was an investment officer at the company for three years. Initially, the investment department was managed by the CEO. Tse is originally from Hong Kong, China. She holds a bachelor's degree in accounting from Golden Gate University in San Francisco and an MBA from California State University, East Bay.

Tse was named on Trusted Insight's 2016 Top 30 Women Chief Investment Officers. She graciously spoke with us on Apr. 11, 2016.

Bill Camelio
Investment Strategist, Yale New Haven Health System

Bill Camelio is an investment strategist at Yale New Haven Health System. Previously, Camelio was a senior associate, senior analyst and analyst at RogersCasey. Prior to that, he was an investment specialist at Prudential Financial. Camelio holds MBA in finance from Northeastern University and a B.A. in finance from Merrimack College.

Camelio was named on Trusted Insight's 2016 Top 30 Hospital Investment Office Rising Stars. He graciously spoke with us on Sep. 22, 2016.

Bob Jacksha
Chief Investment Officer, New Mexico Educational Retirement Board

Bob Jacksha is the chief investment officer of New Mexico Educational Retirement Board, a pension fund with $11 billion assets under management. Prior to being appointed chief investment officer of New Mexico ERB, he was the deputy chief investment officer at the New Mexico State Investment Council. Jacksha holds an MBA from the University of St. Thomas and a bachelor's degree in business administration from Bemidji State University.

Jacksha was named on Trusted Insight's 2016 Top 30 Pension Chief Investment Officers. He graciously spoke with us on Jan. 29, 2016.

Carol McFate
Chief Investment Officer, Xerox

Carol McFate has been the chief investment officer at Xerox since 2006. Her responsibilities include managing over $12 billion in defined benefit and defined contribution investment assets for Xerox's U.S. and U.K. plans. Previously, she was the executive vice president and global treasurer at XL Capital Ltd. Prior to that, she was vice president and treasurer at American International Group. McFate holds an MBA in finance and general management from Harvard Business School and a B.S. in economics, mathematics and music from Juniata College. She is also a Chartered Financial Analyst.

McFate was named on Trusted Insight's 2016 Top 30 Corporate Chief Investment Officers. She graciously spoke with us on Oct. 24, 2016.

Charles Kennedy
Chief Investment Officer, Carnegie Mellon University

Charles Kennedy has been the chief investment officer at Carnegie Mellon University since 2007. Kennedy holds an MBA from Harvard Business School. Previously, he was an investment banker and taught at the University of Pittsburgh.

Kennedy was named on Trusted Insight's 2015 Top 30 Ivy League Graduate Chief Investment Officers. He graciously spoke with us on Oct. 26, 2015.

Chris Ailman
Chief Investment Officer, California State Teachers' Retirement System

Chris Ailman has been the chief investment officer at California State Teachers' Retirement System since 2000. He leads the investment team across private equity, global equity, corporate governance, fixed income, real estate, operations, inflation sensitive and innovation and risk. Previously, he was the chief investment officer of the Washington State Investment Board. Prior to that, he was the chief investment officer at the Sacramento County Employees' Retirement System for 11 years. Ailman holds a bachelor's degree in business economics from the University of California, Santa Barbara. He also received his Certified Financial Planner designation from the University of Southern California.

Ailman was named on Trusted Insight's 2016 Top 30 Pension Fund Chief Investment Officers. He graciously spoke with us on Jan. 26, 2016.

Chris Halaska
Chief Investment Officer, Memorial Hermann Health System

Chris Halaska is senior vice president and chief investment officer at Memorial Hermann Health System. He joined Memorial Hermann in October 2012. Previously, he worked in JPMorgan's investment banking division for more than 12 years. Halaska holds a BBA in finance and an MBA from the University of Texas at Austin.

Halaska was named on Trusted Insight's 2016 Top 30 Hospital Chief Investment Officers. He graciously spoke with us on May 4, 2016.

Colin Ambrose
Chief Investment Officer, UJA-Federation of New York

Colin Ambrose is the chief investment officer at the UJA-Federation of New York, which has $1.4 billion in assets under management. Previously, he was a managing partner at Flexion Asset Management. He holds an MBA from Rensselaer Polytechnic Institute and B.A. from Wesleyan University.

Ambrose was named on Trusted Insight's 2016 Top 30 Endowment Chief Investment Officers. He graciously spoke with Trusted Insight on Mar. 1, 2016.

Courtney Powers
Senior Director of Marketable Alternatives, University of Texas Investment Management Company

Courtney Powers has been the senior director of marketable alternatives at the University of Texas Investment Management Company since 2007. He is responsibility for hedge fund relationships of the University of Texas System's $35 billion endowment pool. Previously, he was a senior associate of mergers and acquisitions at AT&T. Powers holds an MBA in finance from the University of Texas at Austin and a bachelor's degree in English literature from the University of Georgia.

Powers was named on Trusted Insight's 2015 Top 30 University Endowment Investors In Hedge Funds. He graciously spoke with us Sep. 22, 2015.

Craig Robbins
Senior Investment Strategist, Children's Hospitals and Clinics of Minnesota

Craig Robbins is a senior investment strategist at Children's Hospitals and Clinics of Minnesota. He works closely with the hospital's treasurer and provides investment strategy and manager research and performance analysis. In the past, he held multiple project management positions at law and consulting firms. In his earlier career, Robbins was an investment advisor at Merrill Lynch. He received an MBA from the University of Minnesota and a B.A. from Carleton College.

Robbins was named on Trusted Insight's 2016 Top 30 Hospital Investment Office Rising Stars. He graciously spoke with us on Sep. 26, 2016.

Dale Hunt

Manager Director -- Private Equity, Ascension Investment Management

Dale Hunt is managing director of private equity at Ascension Investment Management. Prior to joining Ascension Investment Management, Hunt served as chief investment officer at the West Virginia University Foundation. She was also managing director, global private placements at ABN AMRO and NatWest Markets and held a number of senior investment banking positions at S.G. Warburg, Prudential Securities and Smith Barney.

She began her career on Wall Street in 1978 and has spent over 20 years focusing on private markets. Hunt holds a B.A. in liberal arts from Boston College and an MBA from Pace University.

Hunt was named on Trusted Insight's 2016 Top 30 LPs Investing In Private Equity. She graciously spoke with us on Aug. 31, 2016.

Daniel Parker

Deputy Chief Investment Officers, Texas Tech University

Daniel Parker is the deputy chief investment officer at Texas Tech University. Previously, he was an investment officer at Helmsley Charitable Trust, where he was responsible for strategy development, general research, manager research and portfolio construction in the alternatives and inflation-sensitive segments of the trust's investment program. Prior to that, he was a vice president in private equity at BlackRock and an investment banking associate at Citigroup where he closed more than $20 billion worth of transactions across the capital structure. Parker began his career serving as an officer in the U.S. Marine Corps. He is currently on the board of directors at the Marine Corps Law Enforcement Foundation. He received an MBA from the College of William and Mary and a B.A. from Tulane University.

Parker was named on 2016 Top 30 LP Rising Stars In Venture Capital. He graciously spoke with us on Jan. 13, 2016 while he was at the Helmsley Charitable Trust and on June 14, 2017 as deputy CIO at Texas Tech University.

David Barcus
Manager of Investments, Denison University

David Barcus is the manager of investments at Denison University. He oversees more than $750 million of the university's endowment assets. Previously, he was an investment analyst at the same firm and the vice president in hedge fund manager selection at Amundi Alternative Investments, Inc. for over seven years. Barcus holds an MBA from DePaul University and a B.S. in accounting from Miami University.

David Barcus was named on Trusted Insight's 2016 Top 30 LPs Investing In Credit. He graciously spoke with us on Jul. 13, 2016.

David Erickson
Chief Investment Officer, Ascension Investment Management

David Erickson is the chief investment officer at Ascension Investment Management, where he is responsible for the investment office's administration, management and coordination of investments and operations. Prior to Ascension, he was the chief investment officer of the University of Wisconsin Foundation, a vice president and investment strategist at Strong Capital Management in Wisconsin. Earlier in his career, he was a derivative specialist at PNC Bank/PNC Capital Markets in Pennsylvania, Chemical Bank in New York and Firstar Bank in Wisconsin. Erickson holds a bachelor's degree in economics from Wheaton College. He is also a Chartered Financial Analyst.

Erickson was named on Trusted Insight's 2016 Top 30 Hospital Chief Investment Officers. He graciously spoke with us on May 16, 2016.

David Holmgren
Chief Investment Officer, Hartford HealthCare

David Holmgren is the chief investment officer of Hartford HealthCare in Connecticut. He manages Hartford's $2.2 billion pension, endowment and insurance assets by overseeing risk management, portfolio construction, asset allocation, manager selection and investment operations. Previously, he was a pension investment officer at CT Treasury, an investment consultant at UBS Asset Management and a general partner at LSG. Holmgren holds an MBA from Columbia University and a B.A. in economics and Spanish from Denison University.

Holmgren was named on Trusted Insight's 2015 Top 30 Health Care Institutional Investors. He graciously spoke with us on Dec. 1, 2015.

David Villa
Chief Investment Officer, State of Wisconsin Investment Board

David Villa has been the chief investment officer of the State of Wisconsin Investment Board since 2006. He oversees the state pension's $99 billion in assets. Prior to this, he was the chief investment officer of the Florida State Board of Administration. He also worked for UBS Global Asset Management/Brinson Partners as an executive director and client relationship manager. Villa holds a B.A. in economics from Princeton University, an M.A. in Latin American Studies from Stanford University and an MBA from Northwestern University. He is also a Chartered Financial Analyst.

Villa was named on Trusted Insight's 2016 Top 30 Public Pension Chief Investment Officers. He graciously spoke with us on Nov. 11, 2016.

Dean Duchak
Director of Investments, Kaiser Family Foundation

Dean Duchak is a director of investments at the Kaiser Family Foundation. His responsibilities include assisting in analysis of investment objectives, asset allocation and investment performance, and evaluating existing managers and due diligence on potential investments across a wide range of asset classes. He previously worked as a financial analyst at JPMorgan Chase. Duchak holds a B.S. in finance and accounting from Georgetown University.

Duchak was named on Trusted Insight's 2016 Top 30 Rising Stars At Foundations. He graciously spoke with us on Mar. 24, 2016.

Dhvani Shah
Chief Investment Officer, Illinois Municipal Retirement Fund

Dhvani Shah is the chief investment officer of Illinois Municipal Retirement Fund, a pension fund with $34.9 billion assets under management. Previously, Shah was the managing director of private equity of the $89.9 billion New York State Teachers' Retirement System. Shah has a BBA from Loyola University and an MBA from the University of Chicago Booth School of Business. She is also a Chartered Financial Analyst.

Shah was named on Trusted Insight's 2016 Top 30 Pension Fund Chief Investment Officers and 2017 Top 30 Women Chief Investment Officers. She graciously spoke with us on Jan. 28, 2016 and Feb. 27, 2017.

Elaine Orr
Former Director, Silicon Valley Community Foundation

Elaine Orr served as the director of investments at Silicon Valley Community Foundation from July 2014 to December 2016. She managed the foundation's investment strategy, portfolio transactions, due diligence and investment communications. Prior to that, she was a director of global business development at Morningstar and director of product development at BlackRock. Orr holds a B.Comm in finance from The University of British Columbia. She is also a Chartered Financial Analyst.

Orr was named on Trusted Insight's 2016 Top 30 Foundation Rising Stars. She graciously spoke with us on Tuesday Apr. 13, 2016.

Elizabeth Hewitt
Chief Investment Officer, Alfred P. Sloan Foundation

Elizabeth Hewitt joined the Alfred P. Sloan Foundation in 2015 as chief investment officer and senior vice president. She is responsible for managing the foundation's endowment, including asset allocation strategy, fund manager selection, risk analysis, portfolio performance evaluation and liquidity management. Previously, Hewitt was the managing director of public investments at the Robert Wood Johnson Foundation. Earlier in her career, Hewitt was a senior vice president at Lazard Asset Management, a hedge fund analyst at the Torrey Funds and a wealth management associate at the U.S. Trust Corporation. Hewitt holds a B.A. and an M.A., both from the University of St. Andrews in Scotland. She is a member on the board of directors of the Madeira School in McLean, Virginia, where she chairs the investment committee.

Hewitt was named on Trusted Insight's 2016 Top 30 Women Chief Investment Officers and 2017 Top 30 Foundation Chief Investment Officers. She graciously spoke with us on Mar. 30, 2016.

Eric Kirsch
Global Chief Investment Officer and Executive Vice President, Aflac

Eric Kirsch is the global chief investment officer and executive vice president at Aflac. Previously, he served as managing director and global head of insurance asset management at Goldman Sachs, where he oversaw a global team of 55 people, managing over $70 billion in insurance assets. Prior to that, he spent 27 combined years at Deutsche Asset Management and Bankers Trust Company. Kirsch holds a BBA from Baruch College and an MBA from Pace University. He is also a Chartered Financial Analyst.

Kirsch was named on Trusted Insight's 2016 Top 30 Corporate Chief Investment Officers. He graciously spoke with us on Oct. 24, 2016.

Erik Carleton
Director of Pension Investments, Textron Inc.

Erik Carleton is a director of pension investments at Textron Inc., an industrial conglomerate with $13.4 billion in annual revenue. Carleton manages the global fixed income and public equity investments of the Textron Defined Benefit Plan. He is in charge of the manager selection within public equities, fixed income, currencies and derivatives. His former roles include investment consulting for NEPC and Fiduciary Investment Advisors. He holds an MBA and a Master's in Finance, both from Bentley University. He is also a Chartered Financial Analyst.

Carleton was named on Trusted Insight's 2017 Top 30 Corporate Investment Office Rising Stars. He graciously spoke with us on Mar. 22, 2017.

Erik Lundberg
Chief Investment Officer, University of Michigan

Erik Lundberg has been the chief investment officer at the University of Michigan since 1999. He is responsible for directing the university's $8.5 billion in investment programs. Previously, he was the investment officer for Ameritech. Lundberg holds an MBA in finance and international business from the Ohio State University.

Lundberg was named on Trusted Insight's 2016 Top 30 Endowment Chief Investment Officers. He graciously spoke with us on Mar. 2, 2016.

Geeta Kapadia
Senior Investment Strategist, Yale New Haven Health System

Geeta Kapadia is a senior investment strategist at Yale New Haven Health System. Previously, she was an investment strategist within the same organization. Prior to that, Kapadia was a senior investment consultant at Mercer Investment Consulting and a director of marketing and investment analyst at Capital Metrics & Risk Solutions.

Kapadia holds a master's degree in financial markets and trading from the Illinois Institute of Technology and a bachelor's degree in mathematics from The University of Chicago. She is also a Chartered Financial Analyst.

Kapadia was named on Trusted Insight's 2016 Top 30 Women Rising Stars in Institutional Investing. She graciously spoke with us on Aug. 17, 2016.

Girard Miller
Former Chief Investment Officer, Orange County Employees' Retirement System

Girard Miller served as chief investment officer at the Orange County Employees' Retirement System, a $12 billion defined benefit pension plan, from July 2012 to December 2016. Prior to that, he was a senior strategist at Public Financial Management Group, chief operating officer at Janus Capital Group and President and CEO of ICMA-RC. Miller holds an Master's of Public Administration in finance from Syracuse University. He is also a Chartered FInancial Analyst.

Miller was named on Trusted Insight's 2016 Top 30 Pension Chief Investment Officers. He graciously spoke with us on Jan. 21, 2016.

James Perry
Former Chief Investment Officer, Dallas Police & Fire Pension System

James Perry served as chief investment officer at the Dallas Police & Fire Pension System from September 2015 to July 2016. Prior to that, he was the assistant vice chancellor at Texas Tech University and a senior investment officer at San Bernardino County Employees' Retirement Association. Perry holds an MBA from National University and a bachelor's degree in biochemical and biophysical science from the University of Houston. He also co-published *Dynamic Beta: Getting Paid to Manage Risks* in the Journal of Investment Consulting.

Perry was named to Trusted Insight's 2016 Top 30 Pension Fund Chief Investment Officers. He graciously spoke with us on Jan. 21, 2016.

Jed Johnson
Senior Managing Director, Crow Holdings Capital – Investment Partners

Jed Johnson is a senior managing director and the private markets portfolio manager at Crow Holdings Capital – Investment Partners (CHC-IP), which manages liquid assets for the Trammell Crow family and approximately 30 partner families as an RIA with approximately $2 billion under management. He leads the firm's private markets investment strategy and oversees a team performing private equity manager selection, direct investment evaluation, investment execution and asset management.

Previously, Johnson was a managing director at Parallel Investment Partners, a Dallas-based private equity firm. Before that, he was a vice president at Summit Partners and an associate at Robertson Stephens. Johnson holds a bachelor's degree from Stanford University.

Johnson was named on Trusted Insight's 2016 Top 30 Family Office Rising Stars. He graciously spoke with us on Jun. 17, 2016.

Jennifer Wenzel
Real Estate Investment Manager, The Teacher Retirement System of Texas

Jennifer Wenzel is a real estate investment manager at the Teacher Retirement System of Texas. Wenzel has held various investment positions at the retirement system since February 2009. Prior to that, she was a senior analyst at Cherokee Investment Partners and a financial analyst at Crow Holdings. Wenzel holds a BBA in finance from the University of Texas at Austin.

Wenzel was named on Trusted Insight's 2016 Top 30 Women Rising Stars In Institutional Investing. She graciously spoke with Trusted Insight on Aug. 9, 2016.

Jeremy Wolfson
Chief Investment Officer, Los Angeles Water and Power Employees' Retirement Plan

Jeremy Wolfson is the chief investment officer of Los Angeles Water and Power Employees' Retirement Plan, a $12 billion public pension fund. Previously, he worked for the Los Angeles City Treasurer's Office for two years, where he was responsible for managing the City's $7.5 billion fixed-income portfolio. He was promoted to chief investment officer of the City Treasurer's Office just prior to transferring to the pension plan. Wolfson holds a B.S. in finance from California State University, Northridge and an MBA from Pepperdine University. He is also a member of the CFA Institute and the CAIA Association.

Wolfson was named to Trusted Insight's 2016 Top 30 Penion Chief Investment Officers. He graciously spoke with Trusted Insight on Jan. 19, 2016.

Joel Wittenberg
Chief Investment Officer, W.K. Kellogg Foundation

Joel Wittenberg is the chief investment officer and vice president of the W.K. Kellogg Foundation. He has managed the foundation's $8 billion assets since September 2009. Prior to joining the foundation, Wittenberg served as vice president and treasurer of Kellogg Company and has more than 15 years of experience in global treasury, financial and commodity risk management and pension functions.

Wittenberg was named on Trusted Insight's 2015 Top 30 Foundation Chief Investment Officers. He graciously spoke with us on Nov. 11, 2015.

Jonathan Grabel
Former Chief Investment Officer, Public Employees Retirement Association of New Mexico

Jonathan Grabel is the former chief investment officer of Public Employees Retirement Association of New Mexico from January 2014 to April 2017. He managed the pension fund's $14.5 billion of investment assets. Previously, he was the chief investment officer at Montgomery County Public Schools. Grabel holds an MBA in finance from from The University of Chicago and a B.S. in economics from the University of Pennsylvania -- The Wharton School.

Grabel was named on Trusted Insight's 2016 Top 30 Pension Chief Investment Officers. He graciously spoke with us on Jan. 22, 2016.

Jonathan Hook
Chief Investment Officer, The Harry and Jeanette Weinberg Foundation

Jonathan Hook joined The Harry and Jeanette Weinberg Foundation as its inaugural chief investment officer in May 2014. He oversees the foundation's $2.2 billion of investments across various asset classes. Previously, Hook was the chief investment officer at The Ohio State University from 2008 to 2014 and the chief investment officer at Baylor University from 2001 to 2008. Prior to institutional investing, Hook had a 20-year career in commercial and investment banking. Hook holds a bachelor's degree in economics and sociology from Willamette University and an MBA in finance from Baylor University.

Hook was named on Trusted Insight's 2017 Top 30 Foundation Chief Investment Officers. He graciously spoke with us on Oct. 28, 2015 and Apr. 20, 2017.

Jude Perez
Deputy Chief Investment Officer, New Mexico Public Employees Retirement Association

Jude Perez is the deputy chief investment officer at New Mexico Public Employees Retirement Association. Previously, he served as an investment officer at the same pension for five years. Prior to that, Perez was a snowboard retailer and a land associate at the homebuilding company KB Home, where he gained experience in real estate underwriting. Perez holds an MBA from the University of New Mexico and a B.A. in philosophy from the University of Nevada. He is also a Chartered Alternative Investment Analyst.

Perez was named on Trusted Insight's 2016 Top 30 Future Chief Investment Officers At Pension Funds. He graciously spoke with us on Apr. 21, 2016.

Kathryn Crecelius
Former chief investment officer, Johns Hopkins University

Kathryn Crecelius served as chief investment officer at The Johns Hopkins University's $4 billion endowment from September 2005 to June 2016. Prior to Johns Hopkins, she was a managing director for marketable alternative investments at the Massachusetts Institute of Technology Investment Management Company and a consultant at Cambridge Associates. Crecelius holds a Ph.D. in French literature from Yale University and a B.A. from Bryn Mawr College.

Crecelius was named on Trusted Insight's 2015 Top 30 Women At University Endowments and 2015 Top 30 Ivy League Graduate Chief Investment Officers. She graciously spoke with us on Oct. 23, 2015.

Kathleen Browne
Managing Director, Wellesley College Investment Office

Kathleen Browne is the managing director at Wellesley College. She has been in this role since 2009. Previously, she worked at the Alcatel-Lucent Investment Management Corp. for eight years, most recently serving as the director of alternative investments. She is also a member of the investment committee at Boston Arts Academy and The Foundation for MetroWest. Browne received an MBA from Massachusetts Institute of Technology - Sloan School of Management, a J.D. from Boston College Law School and a B.S. in electrical engineering from Union College.

Browne was named on Trusted Insight's 2016 Top 30 LPs Investing In Real Assets & Real Estate. She graciously spoke with us on Oct. 27, 2016.

Kathleen Vogelsang
Chief Investment Officer, Van Andel Institute

Kathleen Vogelsang is the chief investment officer at Van Andel Institute, a non-profit medical research center based in Grand Rapids, Michigan. Vogelsang joined the institute in 2005 as its inaugural chief investment officer for the organization's $1.3 billion of endowment assets. Previously, Vogelsang was vice president and senior portfolio manager at Fifth Third Bank and an investment manager at JVA Enterprises, a single-family office founded by Amway Corp. co-founder Jay Van Andel and his family. Vogelsang holds a BBA in finance and an MBA from Grand Valley State University. She is a Chartered Financial Analyst.

Vogelsang was named on Trusted Insight's 2017 Top 30 Women Chief Investment Officers. She graciously spoke with us on Feb. 22, 2017.

Kim Lew
Chief Investment Officer, Carnegie Corporation

Kim Lew is vice president and chief investment officer of the Carnegie Corporation of New York, a $3.4 billion private foundation. Previously, Lew managed venture capital, private equity and public equity investments for the Ford Foundation for 13 years. Before Ford, she worked in the Private Placement Group of Prudential and in the Middle Market Banking Group of the former Chemical Bank. Lew holds a B.S in economics from the University of Pennsylvania - The Wharton School and an MBA from Harvard Business School. Lew is also a Chartered Financial Analyst.

Lew was named to Trusted Insight's 2015 Top 30 Foundation Chief Investment Officers. She graciously spoke with us on Oct. 27, 2015. At the time of the interview, Lew was co-chief investment office of Carnegie Corp.

Kimberly Walker
Former Chief Investment Officer, Washington University in St. Louis

Kimberly Walker was the chief investment officer at Washington University in St. Louis from November 2006 to December 2016. She oversaw the investment of the endowment and other assets totaling more than $7 billion. Prior to that, she was president at Qwest Asset Management Company for eight years and the director of equity strategy at General Motors. Walker holds an MBA in finance from the University of Michigan, an M.A. in economics from Washington University in St. Louis and a B.A. in economics from Miami University.

Walker was named on Trusted Insight's 2016 Top 30 Endowment Chief Investment Officers. She graciously spoke with us on Mar. 18, 2016.

Lawrence Kochard
CEO and Chief Investment Officer, University of Virginia Investment Management Company

Lawrence Kochard is the CEO and chief investment officer of the University of Virginia Investment Management Company (UVIMCO), which has $7.5 billion in assets under management. Prior to UVIMCO, he served as the chief investment officer at Georgetown University and the managing director of equity and hedge fund investments at the Virginia Retirement System. Kochard holds an MBA in finance and accounting from the University of Rochester. He also received his M.A. and Ph.D. in economics from the University of Virginia.

Kochard was named on Trusted Insight's 2016 and 2017 Top 30 Endowment Chief Investment Officers. He graciously spoke with us on Mar. 18, 2016 and Feb. 24, 2017.

Linda Calnan
Senior Investment Officer, Houston Firefighters' Relief and Retirement Fund

Linda Calnan is the senior investment officer at Houston Firefighters' Relief and Retirement Fund and manages the pension fund's private equity and real estate portfolios. Previously, Calnan was director of investments of Starling International Management Ltd. based in the United Arab Emirates. She has served on the board of the Institutional Limited Partners Association (ILPA) as its Education Chairperson responsible for the design and curricula stewardship of the ILPA Institute, which was launched under her leadership. She continues to serve the association as a member of its Industry Affairs Committee. Calnan is the Valedictorian of the University of Miami, where she earned her MBA and graduated Summa Cum Laude of Sam Houston State University, where she earned her BBA in economics and international business.

Calnan was named on Trusted Insight's 2016 Top 30 LPs Investing In Private Equity. She graciously spoke with us on Sep. 9, 2016.

Lela Prodani
Senior Investment Analyst, Mercy Health

Lela Prodani is a senior investment analyst at Mercy Health. Previously, she was an investment analyst at the same institution. Prior to that, she was a senior technical products analyst and performance analyst at Mercer and an equity trader and mutual fund specialist at Smith, Moore & Company. Prodani holds a bachelor's degree in international business and an MBA from Webster University. She also holds a Certificate in Investment Performance Measurement.

Prodani was named on Trusted Insight's 2016 Top 30 Women Rising Stars in Institutional Investing. She graciously spoke with us on Aug. 8, 2016.

Lorrie Tingle
Chief Investment Officer, Public Employees' Retirement System of Mississippi

Lorrie Tingle is the chief investment officer of the Public Employees' Retirement System of Mississippi. She has been in this role since 1996, planning and directing the activities for the pension fund's $24 billion investment pool to ensure the prudent management of the investment assets. Tingle holds an MBA from Mississippi College and a bachelor's degree in geology from the University of Alabama.

Tingle was named on Trusted Insight's 2016 Top 30 Public Pension Chief Investment Officers. She graciously spoke with us on Nov. 18, 2016.

Mark Barnard
Former Managing Director of Private Markets, Howard Hughes Medical Institute

Mark Barnard was the managing director of private investments at Howard Hughes Medical Institute's endowment. He left the job in June 2016 after a 20-year tenure. At Howard Hughes, he was responsible for managing the $5 billion private investment portfolio. Prior to that, he was associate director of real estate at MIT and worked in urban planning and development in both the public and the private sectors. Barnard holds a B.A. in urban planning from the University of Cincinnati, a master's degree from Harvard University and has completed course-work in finance as a special student at MIT.

Barnard was named on Trusted Insight's 2015 Top 30 Health Care Institutional Investors. He graciously spoke with us on Dec. 10, 2015.

Mark Canavan
Senior Portfolio Manager, New Mexico Educational Retirement Board

Mark Canavan has been a senior portfolio manager at the New Mexico Education-al Retirement Board for over nine years. His role includes leading the creation, design and implementation of the pension fund's real assets portfolio consisting of real estate, infrastructure, timber, agriculture and mitigation banking asset classes. Since joining, the allocation has grown to $1.7 billion and includes investments in energy, minerals, mining and water. Previously, Canavan was chief investment officer, senior portfolio manager and investment bureau chief at the New Mexico State Treasurer's Office. Canavan studied physics and music at Bard College. He also studied physics at the University of New Mexico.

Canavan was named on Trusted Insight's 2016 Top 30 LPs Investing In Real Estate & Real Assets. He graciously spoke with us on Nov. 4, 2016.

Mark Newcomb
Managing Director - Public Markets, Washington University Investment Management Company

Mark Newcomb is managing director of public markets at Washington University Investment Management Company in St. Louis. Previously, he was a public market manager at the University of Texas Investment Management Company. He has also served as an analyst and portfolio manager for TIAA-CREF's $2.5 billion high-yield group, worked in the equity research department at Bear Stearns and the FAS group at Ernst & Young. Newcomb holds a bachelor's degree in finance from the Texas Christian University and an MBA from UNC Kenan-Flagler Business School. He is also a Chartered Financial Analyst.

Newcomb was named on Trusted Insight's 2016 Top 30 LPs Investing In Credit. He graciously spoke with us on Jul. 12, 2016.

Mark Rich
Director of Investments, Kimbell Art Foundation

Mark Rich is the director of investments at Kimbell Art Foundation, managing the foundation's current portfolio and evaluating future investment opportunities. Previously, he was an audit senior at Ernst & Young. In 2014, Rich won the AICPA Young CPA of the Year Award in honor of Maximo Mukelabai. Rich is currently on the investment committee for both the United Way of Tarrant County and North Texas Community Foundation. Rich holds both a master's in accounting and a bachelor's degree in accounting and finance from Abilene Christian University. He is also a Chartered Financial Analyst and Certified Public Accountant.

Rich was named on Trusted Insight's 2016 Top 30 Rising Stars At Foundations. He graciously spoke with us on Mar. 23, 2016.

Mary Cahill
Chief Investment Officer, Emory University

Mary Cahill has been the vice president of investments and chief investment officer at Emory University for over 16 years. She oversees a $7 billion portfolio of endowment, trust, operating, and employee benefit assets of the University and related medical facilities. Previously, she was deputy chief investment officer of Xerox for 10 years. Cahill has 30 years of investment experience with prior positions in the Virginia Retirement System, SmithKline, BellSouth and Merck pension plans. Cahill holds an MBA in finance from St. John's University.

Cahill was named on Trusted Insight's 2016 Top 30 Women Chief Investment Officers. She graciously spoke with us on Apr. 11, 2016.

Mauricia Geissler
Chief Investment Officer, Amherst College

Mauricia Geissler has been the chief investment officer of Amherst College since 2003, where she manages $2 billion is assets. Prior to Amherst, she was the director of public market investments at Lucent Asset Management and the senior vice president of institutional product strategy and development at Putnam Investments. Geissler holds a B.A. in finance and investments from the University of Wisconsin-Madison's School of Business.

Geissler was named on Trusted Insight's 2016 Top 30 Women Chief Investment officers. She graciously spoke with us on Apr. 18, 2016.

Megan Loehner
Director of Investments, Missouri Local Government Employees Retirement System

Megan Loehner is a director of investments at the Missouri Local Government Employees Retirement System. Previously, she was a senior investment officer at the same institution for over six years. Prior to that, she was an investment officer at the Public School and Education Employee Retirement Systems of Missouri. Loehner holds a bachelor's degree and master's degree, both in accounting, from University of Missouri. She is also a Chartered Financial Analyst, a Chartered Alternative Investment Analyst and a Certified Public Accountant.

Loehner was named on Trusted Insight's 2016 Top 30 Women Rising Stars in Institutional Investing. She graciously spoke to Trusted Insight on Aug. 16, 2016.

Michael Buchman
Co-Chief Investment Officer, The Conrad N. Hilton Foundation

Michael Buchman is the vice president and co-chief investment officer of the Conrad N. Hilton Foundation. In this role, he monitors existing manager relationships and evaluates prospective managers in all asset classes, with primary responsibility for private equity and real estate investments. He also conducts portfolio and strategy analytics. Prior to joining the Hilton Foundation, Buchman worked in the areas of finance, real estate and law at Broadway Partners, Citigroup Global Investment Bank and the law firms of Fried Frank Harris Shriver & Jacobson, and Skadden Arps Slate Meagher & Flom. Buchman received a J.D., an MBA and a B.A. in economics, all from the University of Pennsylvania.

Buchman was named on Trusted Insight's 2016 Top 30 Foundation Rising Stars. He graciously spoke with us on Mar. 31, 2016.

Michael Malewicz
System Vice President of Treasury and Chief Investment Officer, SSM Health

Michael Malewicz is the system vice president – treasury and chief investment officer at SSM Health, a Catholic, not-for-profit health care system. He leads the SSM Health Portfolio Management Company, where he develops capital strategies, leads the issuance of debt, maintains rating agency relationships, continuously enhances the investor relations program, financial modeling and mergers and acquisitions. Prior to joining SSM Health in 2013, Malewicz worked in the treasury and investments departments at several health care systems, including City of Hope in Southern California, Washington Hospital HealthCare System and Swedish Health Services. Prior to his health care career, Malewicz worked in corporate finance at Qualcomm Inc., Quiksilver Inc., and as an investment banker for the Industrial Bank of Japan. Malewicz has an undergraduate degree from San Diego State University and an MBA from University of San Francisco.

Malewicz was named on Trusted Insight's 2017 Top 30 Hospital Investment Officers. He graciously spoke with us on Jan. 25, 2017.

Michael Trotsky
Chief Investment Officer, Massachusetts Pension Reserves Investment Management Board

Michael Trotsky is the executive director and chief investment officer of the Massachusetts Pension Reserves Investment Management Board, a pension fund with $62 billion assets under management. Trotsky's work at the pension fund was preceded by a 25-year career in the private sector, most recently as a senior vice president and portfolio manager at PAR Capital Management. Trotsky received a B.S. in electrical engineering and an MBA from the University of Pennsylvania.

Trotsky was named to Trusted Insight's 2016 Top 30 Pension Fund Chief Investment Officers. He graciously spoke with us on Jan. 21, 2016.

Neal Graziano
Director of Investments, W.K. Kellogg Foundation

Neal Graziano is a director of investments at the W. K. Kellogg Foundation, which manages $3.5 billion in assets. Prior to joining Kellogg in 2007, Graziano was an associate portfolio manager at Mastrapasqua Asset Management and investment analyst at William Blair & Co. Graziano holds a B.A. in finance from Michigan State University and an MBA from the University of Chicago. He is a Chartered Financial Analyst and a Chartered Alternative Investment Analyst Designations.

Graziano was named on Trusted Insight's 2016 Top 30 LPs Investing Real Assets, Real Estate. He graciously spoke with us on Nov. 1, 2016.

Novisi Nirschl
Director of Private Investments, Memorial Sloan-Kettering Cancer Center

Novisi Nirschl is the director of private investments at the investment office of Memorial Sloan-Kettering Cancer Center. She oversees private equity and real asset investments for the endowment. Previously, Nirschl was a vice president at Fortress Investment Group, where she primarily made investments in private equity and real asset funds and co-investments for the Fortress Partners Fund in New York. Nirschl holds an MBA from Stanford University and a B.A. from Harvard College.

Novisi Nirschl was named on Trusted Insight's 2016 Top 30 Health Care Institutional Investors. She graciously spoke with us on Jan. 11, 2016.

Philip Rotner
Chief Investment Officer, Boston Children's Hospital

Philip Rotner is the inaugural chief investment officer at Boston Children's Hospital, where he has served since 2010. He manages the organization's endowment, pension and short-term investment assets, as well as hiring and developing a top-tier investment team. Previously, he was the managing director of MIT Investment Management Company for more than 17 years. Rotner holds an MBA in finance from the University of Chicago and a B.A. in economics from Amherst College.

Rotner was named on Trusted Insight's 2017 Top 30 Hospital Investment Officers. He graciously spoke with us on Jan. 17, 2017.

Renee Hanna
Director of Investments, Baylor University

Renee Hanna has been the director of investments at Baylor University since 2008. Previously, she was an associate investment strategist at Lee Financial Corporation, a multi-family investment office. She is responsible for the investment and management of the private equity and real asset allocations. Hanna holds a BBA in finance from Baylor University and an associate of arts from Mclennan Community College. She is also a Chartered Financial Analyst.

Hanna was named on Trusted Insight's 2016 Top 30 Female Limited Partners In Private Equity. She graciously spoke with us on Feb. 16, 2016.

Robert C. Lee III
Former Investment Director, Employees Retirement System of Texas

Robert C. Lee III is the former investment director of hedge funds at the Employees Retirement System of Texas, where he oversaw the $26 billion pension fund's hedge funds, liquid alternatives and hybrid investments. Before that, he was an associate director of portfolio management for Riverside Portfolio Management and HFR Asset Management. Lee left the pension in September 2016 to join Texas Tech University as the university endowment's deputy chief investment officer.

Lee holds a bachelor's degree in mathematics and economics from Texas State University and a master's in econometrics, international financial management from University of Konstanz. Lee is a certified hedge fund professional and a Chartered Financial Analyst.

Lee was named on Trusted Insight's 2016 Top 30 LPs Investing In Hedge Funds. He graciously spoke with us on Jul. 12, 2016, prior to leaving the pension fund.

Robert Maynard
Chief Investment Officer, Public Employee Retirement System of Idaho

Robert Maynard is the chief investment officer of the Public Employee Retirement System of Idaho, a pension with $15 billion in assets under management. Previously he served as deputy executive director of the Alaska Permanent Fund. Maynard graduated from Claremont Men's (now Claremont McKenna) College and received his J.D. from the University of California, Davis School of Law.

Maynard was named on Trusted Insight's 2016 Top 30 Public Pension Chief Investment Officers. He graciously spoke with us on Jan. 18, 2016 and Nov. 14, 2016.

Rob Roy
Chief Investment Officer, Adventist Health System

Rob Roy is the chief investment officer at Adventist Health System. Previously, he was the chief investment officer at Cain Brothers Asset Management and initially a director of investments at Adventist Health System. Roy holds a bachelor's degree in applied mathematics from Southern New Hampshire University and a master's in financial markets and trading from the Illinois Institute of Technology.

Roy was named on Trusted Insight's 2016 Top 30 Hospital Chief Investment Officers. He graciously spoke with us on May 23, 2016.

Rodney Overcash
Investment Director, Margaret A. Cargill Philanthropies

Rodney Overcash is the investment director of credit strategies at Margaret A. Cargill Philanthropies. His role includes planning and implementing credit strategies for each of the three grant making entities that make up the Philanthropies: Margaret A. Cargill Foundation, Anne Ray Charitable Trust and Akaloa Resource Foundation. Previously, he was the investment director at North Carolina Investment Management and the direct of research at Marquette Associates. Overcash holds an MBA in analytic finance, econometrics and statistics from the University of Chicago and a B.A. in economics and international studies from the University of North Carolina.

Overcash was named on Trusted Insight's 2016 Top 30 Foundation Rising Stars. He graciously spoke with us on Mar. 23, 2016.

Ron Virtue
Director of Investments, JM Family Enterprises

Ron Virtue is the director of investments at JM Family Enterprises, a diversified automotive company headquartered in Deerfield Beach, Florida. The firm is a distributor for Toyota and Lexus automobiles in the U.S. market. Virtue has been with JM Family Enterprises since 2004, first as an investment analyst and gradually worked his way up. Now as the director of investments, he monitors and provides recommendations for the company's various investment pools, including its retirement plans, 401(k) plan and other portfolios. Virtue received a B.S. in mathematics and statistics from the University of Michigan and an MBA from the University of Chicago.

Virtue was named on Trusted Insight's 2016 Top 30 Corporate Chief Investment Officers. He graciously spoke with us on Nov. 4, 2016.

Sam Masoudi
Chief Investment Officer, Wyoming Retirement System

Sam Masoudi is the chief investment officer at the Wyoming Retirement System, where he oversees the defined benefit and deferred compensation programs. Previously, he was the managing director for investments at Tulane University and the founder and portfolio manager at Silver Peak Capital Management. Masoudi holds a B.S. in finance and investments from Babson College. He is currently an endowment committee member and pension plan committee member at the Logan School for Creative Learning. He also a Chartered Financial Analyst and a Chartered Alternative Investment Analyst.

Masoudi was named on Trusted Insight's 2016 Top 30 Pension Fund Chief Investment Officers. He graciously spoke with us on Jan. 28, 2016.

Sean Feng
Director of Investments, Kresge Foundation

Sean Feng is the director of the investment office at the Kresge Foundation, a $3.6 billion private foundation based in Michigan. Before joining Kresge in 2011, Feng was an equity portfolio manager. He began his career conducting fundamental stock research for Citigroup Investment Research and later worked as an equity analyst covering U.S. small- and mid-cap stocks in a money management firm.

Feng moved to the United States after college to pursue a Ph.D. degree in pharmacology, but soon found himself fascinated with finance and investing. He discontinued his Ph.D. study in pharmacology and instead pursued an MBA. He holds an MBA from the University of Chicago and a M.S. from the University of Texas.

Feng was named on Trusted Insight's 2016 Top 30 Foundation Rising Stars. He graciously spoke with us on Mar. 29, 2016.

Scott Davis
Chief Investment Officer, Indian Public Retirement System

Scott Davis is the chief investment officer of the Indiana Public Retirement System, a pension fund with approximately $30.7 billion in assets under management. He was appointed interim chief investment from September 2015 and officially assumed the role in June 2016. Previously, he was the deputy chief investment officer and the director of public equity at the pension fund. Davis received a B.S. with honors in accounting and finance from Indiana University.

Davis was named on Trusted Insight's 2016 Top 30 Public Pension Chief Investment Officers. He graciously spoke with us on Nov. 22, 2016.

Shawn Egan
Chief Investment Officer, Antares Capital Partners

Shawn Egan is a general partner and chief investment officer at Antares Capital Partners, a single-family office. Previously, he was managing principal at Eamon Advisory LLC, a director of investments at Fine Family Office and director of research at Deloitte & Touche Investment Advisors. In 2004, he jointly-published an article titled *Evaluating and Classifying Taxable Account Managers* in the Journal of Wealth Management. Egan holds an MBA from the University of Massachusetts at Amherst and a B.S. in finance from Fairfield University. He is also a Chartered Financial Analyst.

Egan was named on Trusted Insight's 2016 Top 30 Family Office Rising Stars. He graciously spoke with us on Jun. 20, 2016.

Steve Edmundson
Investment Officer, Public Employees' Retirement System of Nevada

Steve Edmundson is the investment officer at the Public Employees' Retirement System of Nevada. As a one-man team, he oversees all aspects of the system's $34.9 billion investment program, including investment operations, compliance, research, manager oversight and implementation of investment strategy.

Edmundson was named on Trusted Insight's 2016 Top 30 Public Pension Chief Investment Officers. He graciously spoke with us on Nov. 15, 2016.

Steve Groves
Investment Officer, The University of Rochester

Steve Groves has been the investment officer at the University of Rochester since 2000, where he is responsible for the endowment's real assets holdings. Previously, he worked in the risk department at Manning & Napier. Groves holds a B.S. and B.A. from State University of New York at Fredonia and an MBA from the University of Rochester.

Groves was named on Trusted Insight's Top 30 Real Estate Investors At Endowments. He graciously spoke with us on May 31, 2016.

Stuart Mason
Chief Investment Officer, University of Minnesota

Stuart Mason is the associate vice president and chief investment officer at the University of Minnesota, which has $3.3 billion of investment assets under management. Previously, he spent 15 years as a senior investment banker and executive officer in several investment banks including Dougherty Company, EVEREN Securities and Dain Rauscher Corporation. He also served for 10 years as a vice president of Wells Fargo Corporation. Mason holds an MBA in business from the University of Minnesota and a B.A. in chemistry and biology from St. Olaf College.

Mason was named on Trusted Insight's 2016 and 2017 Top 30 Endowment Chief Investment Officers. He graciously spoke with us on Mar. 8, 2016.

Thomas Masthay
Director of Real Assets, Texas Municipal Retirement System

Tom Masthay is the director of real assets at Texas Municipal Retirement System. Previously, he was a principal investment analyst at NextEra Energy Inc. and a director of real assets at Kentucky Retirement Systems. Masthay holds an MBA in finance and a BBA in finance and economics from the University of Kentucky. In 2012, he jointly-published an article titled *Considerations Around Placements Agents* in the Journal of Private Equity.

Masthay was named on Trusted Insight's 2016 Top 30 LPs Investing In Real Assets, Real Estate. He graciously spoke with us on Nov. 8, 2016.

Yup Kim
Senior Portfolio Manager, Alaska Permanent Fund Corporation

Yup Kim is a senior portfolio manager of special opportunities at the Alaska Permanent Fund Corporation, a $54 billion sovereign wealth fund. The flexible mandate, which represents 20 percent of the fund's assets, focuses on situations stemming from supply and demand imbalances, capital flight, structural complexities or unique opportunities with asymmetric payoffs and covers a wide spectrum including directly sourced venture capital and private equity transactions, GP co-investments and strategic stakes and partnerships with investment management firms. Previously, Kim was a vice president and investment committee member at Deutsche Bank. Prior to that, he held positions at Performance Equity, Silver Point Capital and Citigroup. Kim holds a B.A. in economics and architecture from Yale University.

Kim was named on Trusted Insight's 2016 Top 30 Sovereign Wealth Fund Rising Stars. Trusted Insight interviewed him via email communications on Sep. 28, 2016.

Acknowledgments

To the institutional investment community: Thank you for speaking with Trusted Insight; sharing your knowledge and experiences; and making Trusted Insight the world's largest network of institutional investors. It is truly an honor to pick your brains and hear your stories. This book would not be possible without your kindness and intellectual contributions.

To Lawrence E. Kochard: We deeply appreciate the time you took from your busy schedule to write an insightful foreword for this book. In our discussions, you have been candid, thought-provoking and an all-around joy to speak with.

To the Trusted Insight team: A great deal of time and energy was exerted in this project, and every team member deserves immense gratitude for their work behind the scenes, in front of institutional investors and through long hours in the office. If not for Daria Shamrai, Hannah Cho, Milton Urgiles, Christina Zhang, Andrew Dombrowski, James Bowa, Rachel Schmulevich and Becky Nye, there would be no book, no interviews and no beautiful images. Thank you so much for your contributions.

To Alex Bangash & Eugene Lebedev: Thank you for having the faith and foresight in your staff to represent the Trusted Insight brand, build relationships with institutional investors and produce quality, meaningful insights on the industry.

About Trusted Insight

Trusted Insight is the world's biggest network of institutional investors. We provide investment decision-makers at endowments, foundations, pensions, insurance companies, sovereign wealth funds, family offices, corporations and health care systems with access to a global professional network, alternative investment opportunities and an informational advantage in private markets.

www.ingramcontent.com/pod-product-compliance
Lightning Source LLC
Chambersburg PA
CBHW070514200326
41519CB00013B/2806